ACETARIA

A DISCOURSE OF SALLETS

The Rusticall and Œconomical Works of

JOHN EVELYN

ACETARIA
A DISCOURSE OF SALLETS
(1699)

General editor CHRISTOPHER DRIVER
with an introduction by Tom Jaine

PROSPECT BOOKS
1996

Published by Prospect Books in 1996,
at Allaleigh House, Blackawton, Totnes, Devon TQ9 7DL.

A CIP record for this book is available from the British Library.

©1996, foreword, Christopher Driver
©1996, introduction and editorial matter, Tom Jaine

The description 'Rusticall and Œconomical' derives from Evelyn's
own description of such books in his library catalogue.

ISBN 0907325645

Printed by The Cromwell Press, Broughton Gifford, Wiltshire.

CONTENTS

FOREWORD

A S I look at the nine volumes of the diary of Samuel Pepys, and the five of John Evelyn's, both superbly indexed in our own time, I question how we could see or hear the period better: King Charles's execution and the decade of the Commonwealth; the Restoration and his son's numerous whores, created duchesses; the Royal Society, architecture and the beginnings of the Enlightenment; and not least, the food and drink, and domestic manners, of a generation of Londoners. Neither diarist would have thought the small details of their lives so imperishable after three centuries.

In beginning a short sequence of John Evelyn's own writings on matters of food and the garden, how better to give it impetus than by re-issuing *Acetaria*? It encapsulates Evelyn's ability to invest the everyday with an apparently insupportable burden of classical allusion and scholarship. Yet given a short moment of absorption and contemplation, his arguments are seductive and provoking, and his instructions clear — and well founded in practice and experience.

Just how well founded will be the more obvious when the next volume in this series is published. *John Evelyn, Cook* is a transcript of his manuscript recipe book, which contains the originals of many of the recipes contained in the Appendix to *Acetaria*.

Christopher Driver

INTRODUCTION

JOHN Evelyn (1620–1706) was the second son of a Surrey squire, Richard Evelyn of Wotton—himself one of the twenty four children of George Evelyn, a manufacturer of gunpowder and patent holder in the reign of Elizabeth I. His childhood was spent largely in the protective care of his maternal step-grandmother, at Lewes in Sussex, where his education was, by his own account, 'extreamely remisse', before he was enrolled at the Middle Temple in 1636 and Balliol College, Oxford, in the following year.

Evelyn spent much of his life avoiding practical and political unpleasantness, a quietist by nature, though displaying persistent devotion to the Anglican church and an almost puritan sense of morality, most often voiced in his animadversions on the profanity of life at Court, evinced too in his dismissal of his errant daughter Elizabeth, and teasingly displayed in his fervent yet platonic relationship with Margaret Blagge. When faced with the unwelcome choices of civil war, he did the right thing by volunteering for the King's service in 1642, but the wise in returning to Wotton immediately the royalists retreated from the London region. His first act while riding out the storm at his brother's house was to construct an island retreat 'in a tyme of so great jealosy'—his first piece of gardening. This proved insufficient protection from the attentions of Parliament men: he wrote in his diary—in its own way as revealing as Samuel Pepys's—'The Covenant being pressed, I absented my selfe… finding it impossible to evade the doing of very unhandsome things…which had been a great Cause of my perpetuall motions hitherto betweene Lond: and Wotton:' And so he left on an extended European tour.

John Evelyn is described as a virtuoso: a man of talent and wide interests, who applied them as he saw fit, without the burden of necessity or outside direction. Self-imposed exile in Europe during much of the Civil War ensured he possessed no mere insular sensibility, just as exile during the Commonwealth was to shape the intellectual tilt of the Restoration court later in the century. Part of Evelyn's virtuosity was to interpret these continental lessons— whether in gardening, sculpture and engraving, architecture, design or applied science— for the English at large.

✳ ✳ ✳ ✳

So far as readers of the present work are concerned, details of his life are of little relevance. In brief, he married Mary, the only, and very young, daughter of the English ambassador to France, Sir Richard Browne, in 1647 in Paris before returning alone to England, eventually settling at Sayes Court in Deptford, the property of his father-in-law from whom he was to purchase it in 1653. He remained here until 1694, when he moved to Wotton at the request of his elder brother, to whom he was heir-apparent.

Once the period of his travels—in the Low Countries, France, and Italy—was definitively over in 1652, Evelyn divided his time between Deptford, London and, after 1660, the court. He held certain public appointments, most notably Commissioner for Sick and Wounded Sea-men and Prisoners of War from 1664, Councillor on Plantations from 1671, culminating in his joining in the Commission for the Privy Seal while the Lord Privy Seal, Lord Clarendon, served as Lord Lieutenant in Ireland in 1685. But while he was assiduous in the performance of his duties, his chief concerns revolved more around the foundation and protection of the fledgling Royal Society, of which he was Secretary in 1672, and proffering advice on matters of art and architecture to the government, for instance in the restoration of St Paul's or the building of the Hospital at Greenwich.

At Sayes Court he enlarged and nurtured the gardens, particularly during the years of the Interregnum when public employment was denied him. When Samuel Pepys visited in 1665, he remarked that they were, 'for variety of evergreens and hedge of holly, the finest things I ever saw in my life.' This was the hedge that Czar Peter was later to delight in being pushed through in a wheelbarrow when tenant in 1698. Pepys records on that same day that he travelled with Evelyn to Greenwich, 'all the way having fine discourse of trees and the nature of vegetables', a preoccupation that resurfaced in *Acetaria* thirty four years later.

Evelyn was a prolific writer and translator, touching on politics, manners and religion as well as the more practical arts of architecture, painting and engraving, sculpture, numismatics, gardening and forestry. His most important original contributions are perhaps *Sylva*, 'a Discourse of Forest Trees' (as *Acetaria* was subtitled 'A Discourse of Sallets'), which he composed at the behest of the Royal Society in 1664 and which went into three subsequent editions gaining further additions such as his *Terra*, 'a Philosophical Discourse of Earth' (1675), *Pomona*, 'an Appendix concerning Fruit-trees' (1664), and *Kalendarium Hortense; Or; Gard'ners Almanac* (1664). These would have been overshadowed by his projected great work *Elysium Britannicum*, which is foreshadowed in the table of contents headed *The Plan of a Royal Garden* printed as a preface to *Acetaria*. *Kalendarium Hortense*, *Terra*, and *Acetaria* were to have been but chapters in this much longer book.

Part and parcel of his literary exploration of the garden were his translations of the French horticultural manual by Nicholas de Bonnefons and the garden poem (in Latin) by Renatus Rapinus

(René Rapin) as well as the introduction to de la Quintenye's *Compleat Gardener*, even if the translation is no longer thought to be Evelyn's. These, like the tenor of his advice to people on garden design and planting, were important elements in his mediation of the European experience and English sensibilities. *Acetaria* is certainly full of observation of how English practise, either in the garden or at table, differed from French, Italian and Spanish—with occasional reference to India, Germany, Holland, Africa and America for good measure. The text also underscores the relative novelty of some aspects of the art of kitchen-gardening in England: we had much to learn by way of cultural techniques from the Dutch and the French, as well as plants that were of recent introduction, for example the Dutch cabbages brought over by Sir Anthony Ashley.

There are practical reasons why Evelyn might have written a book about salads and saladings so late in his life. He had only recently taken up residence at Wotton and the book may reflect his designs for improvement of the kitchen garden there. For sure, he was still actively engaged in agriculture once he took over the running of the estate on his brother's demise. He also retained a watching brief for the prosperity of the Royal Society, and the dedication reflects his urge to use every opportunity open to him for pressing its claims—this time for permanent quarters for its meetings and collections (not least of much of his own literary output).

But that *Acetaria* reflects a lifelong interest in horticulture and production for the table is also inescapable. The directions for the gardener at Sayes Court, published in 1932 by Geoffrey Keynes, reveal a man already well versed in growing for the kitchen. His report to the Royal Society on the extreme weather conditions of

1684 gives further evidence of the practical tilt to his gardening. Among the exotics such as cork trees, arbutus and pomegranate, he lost his rosemary, 'to my great sorrow, because I had not only beautiful hedges of it, but sufficient to afford me flowers for the making a very considerable quantity of the Queen of Hungaries celebrated water.' Victim too was the sea purslain [*Atriplex portulacoides*], 'of which I had a pretty hedge', but most of his vegetables and saladings survived, 'except artichokes, which are universally lost, and (what I prefer before any sallad eaten raw when young) my sampier is all rotted to the very root. How to repair my loss I know not, for I could never make any of the seed which came from the rock sampire, though mine were of the very kind to grow.'

What comes over most forcibly in the book as we have it is a wish to educate. Evelyn had several arrows to his quiver of argument; perhaps too many, for clarity is often sacrificed to an interesting diversion. On one level the book is introducing English palates to a new range of foodstuffs, which has a consequence on the order of meals and the courses within them; on another, there is an enquiry into the general effect of the diet of man on his nature; while a third records impressions and observations of the effect on health of certain foodstuffs; and finally there is an attempt to place this part of our diet in the context of classical and early Christian experience, a form of gastronomic humanism.

The American scholar T. Sarah Peterson has outlined the transition from the sweet-savoury flavours of medieval Europe, delighting in golden colouring and heady, spiced perfumes, to the more naturalistic range of tastes introduced in Italy and France from the sixteenth century that was the foundation of the modern palate. This modern cookery, for want of a better term, derived from a strict separation of sweet and savoury, and had at its heart the 'salt-acid taste', 'whether is was a platter of salt meat, a composite dish with pickled products, a grand salad—almost a meal in itself—or...the entire meal, in fact, up to the dessert.'

Acetaria, which means, literally, 'sallets, or herbs mixed with vinegar to stir up appetite', according to *A Physical Dictionary* of 1657, falls happily into this general scheme, and is equally well-suited in particulars, for instance Evelyn's espousal of the cause of capers—an important signifier of the 'movement' in Peterson's view—and his emphasis on pickles in the appendix of recipes.

A necessary adjunct of refashioning acceptable flavours and patterns of eating was to seek intellectual support from classical literature. Peterson includes a quotation from Rabelais that encapsulates this project: 'They began to converse daily together, speaking in the first place of the virtues, properties, efficacy, and nature of whatever was served to them at table: of the bread, the wine, the water, the salt, the meats, fish, fruit, herbs and roots, and of their dressing. From this talk Gargantua learned in a very short time all the relevant passages in Pliny, Athenaeus, Dioscorides, Julius Pollux, Galen, Porphyrius, Oppian, Polybius, Heliodorus, Aristotle, Aelian, and others. As they held these conversations they often had the aforementioned books brought to table, to make sure of their quotations.' This is mirror image of Evelyn's literary technique.

Evelyn brought his own Christian education to reinforce this tactic—he had, after all, translated St John Chrysostom as well as Lucretius—but his reliance on patristic literature was part of his wider exploration of morality in eating: whether man was meant to be carnivorous; how far food pandered to excess and bestiality; where lay the golden mean in consumption; matters he subjected to reference to the bible, the Christian fathers, classical authority and history, as well as to more empirical studies by contemporaries such as John Ray or Martin Lister.

If, as a fellow of the Royal Society, he was prepared to embrace the new science, his book showed little deviation from the classical doctrine of the humours, save in his concern for preventives of scurvy, when describing the effects of each salad plant. References to Galen are exceeded only by those to Athenaeus and Pliny.

A book about the glories of the salad was perhaps the ideal place to discuss the virtue of abstaining from meat. Evelyn rehearses arguments that had been current for much of the seventeenth century, from the biblical prohibition of eating blood, to the denial of meat by Pythagoras, the propensity of carnivores to violence, the equal intelligence and greater longevity of vegetarians, the acceptance by modern scientists that man was not carnivorous by nature or physiology, and the horrors of contemporary slaughterhouses and butchers' premises. But he was not himself a vegetarian and he appears to use the debate as a means to condemn excess and luxury, condemning strong drink and strong sauces in one breath, usually coupled with improvident greed—hence his praise of the emperor Tacitus satisfied with 'a sallet and a single pullet', while the beastly Maximinus, '(a profess'd enemy to sallet) is reported to have scarce been satisfied, with sixty pounds of flesh, and drink proportionable.' Frugality is equated with a natural appetite, and an honest meal is defined as 'without so much as a grain of exotic spice'. This agrees with Evelyn's analogy of composing a salad with harmonies in music: the counterbalancing of natural flavours with judicious seasoning from a restricted range of condiments, affirmed by the quotation from the Greek dramatist Cratinus on the title-page, 'It is in every man's power to season well.'

Acetaria is not the workaday horticultural instruction that was Evelyn's *Kalendarium Hortense*. Sub-title is accurate reflection of the contents. Nor is it a simple cookery book: the recipes are largely confined to the ghetto of an appendix. But practicalities are not wholly sacrificed to intellectual discourse, and the curious reader could glean some instruction for purposes of cultivation, just as the cook might profit from the details of composition, flavour harmonies and processing.

That Evelyn was himself interested in kitchen matters will be forcibly demonstrated by the forthcoming transcript of his manuscript recipe collection, as if there was not proof enough in the text of *Acetaria*. He had encountered the mixed genre of cookery and gardening before, while translating Nicolas de Bonnefons' *Le Jardinier françois* (published in France in 1651) for the English market in 1658. This was less avowedly a cookery book than its successor *Les Delices de la campagne*, but nonetheless had many recipes for preserving and candying fruit. In his translation, Evelyn omitted them, justifying his action 'because it is a mysterie that I am little acquainted withall; and that I am assured by a lady, who is a person of quality, and curious in that art, that there is nothing extraordinary amongst them, but what the fair sex do infinitely exceed, whenever they please to divertise themselves in that *sweet* employment.' He went on to remark (in the preface to his second edition of 1669) that Bonnefons had produced an excellent cookery book which told how to prepare and serve foods *à la mode de France*, 'which such as affect more then I, and do not understand in the original, may procure to be interpreted, but by some better hand then he that did the "French Cook;" which being (as I am informed) an excellent book of its kinde, is miserably abused for want of skill in the kitchen.' This is reference to the English translation of La Varenne that appeared in two editions in 1653 and 1654.

Bonnefons might not always have approved of Evelyn, for he condemns authors 'who make use of the subject rather to display the strength of their genius than to give some kind of instruction', but the translation places the Englishman in the mainstream of new thinking about flavours and cookery (albeit of a simpler kind than the elaborate court cookery described by La Varenne). 'The Third Book,' Bonnefons writes in *Les Delices de la campagne*, 'has as its subject the real flavour which should be given to each kind of flesh and fish, which the majority of your cooks do not study. So preoccupied are they with the good opinion which people have of their abilities that they imagine that so long as they disguise and garnish their dishes in confusion they will pass for clever men.' These are sentiments echoed by John Evelyn in *Acetaria*.

Evelyn maintained a fiction in his appendix of recipes that he received them from 'an experienc'd housewife'. Comparison with his own manuscript recipe book shows that many of the pickles, for example, were already noted in his own collection, and the text in *Acetaria* is mere rephrasing of recipes he had possessed for many years. Like his friend Sir Kenelm Digby, he was no slouch in kitchen affairs—prepared to experiment (as in his macaroons that substituted sunflower seeds for almonds) and to record.

ACKNOWLEDGEMENTS, AND A NOTE ON SOURCES

The master text of Evelyn's diary is edited by E.S. de Beer, *The Diary of John Evelyn*, 6 vols., Oxford 1955. A more recent version in a single volume, omitting reports of sermons but including most other relevant material, is *The Diary of John Evelyn*, edited by Guy de la Bédoyère, Headstart History, Bangor, 1994. The bibliography is a useful starting place for further study of John Evelyn's life and works. The same editor has produced a single volume compendium of Evelyn's miscellaneous writings, *The Writings of John Evelyn*, Boydell Press, 1995. This includes *Sylva*, *Kalendarium Hortense*, *Fumifugium* and *London Redivivum*. More of his works, including *Acetaria*, are included in the large volume *The Miscellaneous Writings of John Evelyn, Esq. F.R.S.*, edited by William Upcott in 1825. A full bibliography is that by G.L. Keynes, *John Evelyn: a study in bibliophily & a bibliography of his writings*, Cambridge 1937, second edition Oxford 1968.

Material for this introduction has been obtained from Barbara Ketcham Wheaton, *Savouring the Past, the French Kitchen and Table from 1300 to 1789*, London 1983; T. Sarah Peterson, *Acquired Taste, the French Origins of Modern Cooking*, Cornell 1994; and Keith Thomas, *Man and the Natural World*, London 1983.

I am grateful to Maggie Black for her observations and contributions towards understanding Evelyn.

A NOTE ON THE PRESENT EDITION

The text which is transcribed is that of 1699, reprinted in facsimile by Prospect Books in 1982. Although there are no omissions by design, nor variations in spelling or punctuation (in the main text), the use of italics has been altered to conform with modern convention and make a difficult text more readable. Capital letters have also been suppressed to agree current usage, though Evelyn often used the colon as we would use the full stop. Any modern interpolations are enclosed by square brackets.

On the pages following are reproduced in facsimile Evelyn's table of salad plants and their consumption through the seasons of the year, drawn up in consultation with the scientist Robert Boyle and the gardener George London. It was placed at the end of the section entitled 'Furniture and Materials' in the original edition, that is, between pages 58 and 59 of the present edition.

Greek script has been transliterated (and where necessary translated) on the grounds that few people today read Greek with the facility of John Evelyn. I am grateful to John Wilkins of the University of Exeter for providing these. The transliterations are printed in small capitals to distinguish them from other languages.

The footnotes contain many editorial extensions, in square brackets, of Evelyn's abbreviated entries, and the original punctuation has been altered to make them more understandable. Although every effort has been made to identify authors and works cited, the accuracy or otherwise of Evelyn's references and quotations—he was notoriously haphazard, relying on memory—have not been tested.

Evelyn's original index has been included, with the references adjusted to agree with the current text. A further, modern index and glossary has been added. This elucidates obscure words, gives a fuller listing of plants, together with their botanical names, and indexes authors, but not their books, cited by Evelyn.

CAVEAT
John Evelyn had abounding curiosity, and perhaps a strong stomach. It behoves the modern publisher to warn against trials of every foodstuff mentioned in the original text, some may prove toxic.

The Table of plants and the composition of salads.

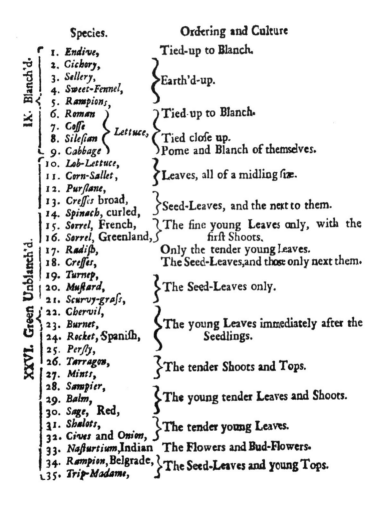

	Species.	Ordering and Culture
IX. Blanch'd.	1. *Endive,*	Tied-up to Blanch.
	2. *Cichory,*	
	3. *Sellery,*	Earth'd-up.
	4. *Sweet-Fennel,*	
	5. *Rampions,*	
	6. *Roman* }	Tied-up to Blanch.
	7. *Coffe* } *Lettuce,*	
	8. *Silefian* }	Tied clofe up.
	9. *Cabbage* }	Pome and Blanch of themselves.
XXVI. Green Unblanch'd.	10. *Lob-Lettuce,*	Leaves, all of a midling fize.
	11. *Corn-Sallet,*	
	12. *Purflane,*	
	13. *Creffes* broad,	Seed-Leaves, and the next to them.
	14. *Spinach,* curled,	
	15. *Sorrel,* French,	The fine young Leaves only, with the
	16. *Sorrel,* Greenland,	firft Shoots.
	17. *Radifh,*	Only the tender young Leaves.
	18. *Creffes,*	The Seed-Leaves, and thofe only next them.
	19. *Turnep,*	
	20. *Muftard,*	The Seed-Leaves only.
	21. *Scurvy-grafs,*	
	22. *Chervil,*	
	23. *Burnet,*	The young Leaves immediately after the
	24. *Rocket,* Spanifh,	Seedlings.
	25. *Perfly,*	
	26. *Tarragon,*	The tender Shoots and Tops.
	27. *Mints,*	
	28. *Sampier,*	The young tender Leaves and Shoots.
	29. *Balm,*	
	30. *Sage,* Red,	
	31. *Shalots,*	The tender young Leaves.
	32. *Cives* and *Onion,*	
	33. *Nafturtium,* Indian	The Flowers and Bud-Flowers.
	34. *Rampion,* Belgrade,	The Seed-Leaves and young Tops.
	35. *Trip-Madame,*	

Month.	Order and Cult.	Species.	Proportion.
January,	Blanch'd as before	Rampions, Endive, Succory, Fennel, sweet. Sellery,	10 2 5 } Roots in Number. 10 4
		Lamb-Lettuce, Lob-Lettuce, Radish, Cresses, Turneps,	A pugil of each.
February		Mustard Seedlings, Scurvygrass, Spinach,	Three parts each.
	Green and Unblanch'd	Sorrel, Greenland, Sorrel, French, Chervil, sweet,	Of each One part.
		Burnet, Rocket,	Two parts.
and		Tarragon, Balm, Mint, Sampier, Shalots,	One part of each.
		Cives,	Twenty large Leaves.
March.		Cabbage-Winter.	One small part of each.
April,	Blanch'd	Lop, Silesian Winter Lettuce, Roman Winter Lettuce,	Very few.
		Radishes, Cresses,	Two pugils or small handfuls.
May,	Green-Herbs Unblanch'd	Cresses, Purslain, Sorrel, French, Sampier,	Of each a pugil. Three parts. Two parts. 1 Fasciat, or pretty full gripe. Two parts. One part.
and	Note, That the young Seedling Leaves of O-range and Li-mon may all these Months be mingled with the Salet.	Onions, young, Sage-tops, the Red, Parsley, Cresses, the Indian, Lettuce, Belgrade, Trip-Madame,	Six parts. Two parts. Of each One part.
June.		Chervil, sweet Burnet,	Two parts.
July,	Blanch'd, and may be eaten by themselves with some Nasturtium-Flower.	Silesian Lettuce, Roman Lettuce, Cress, Cabbage, Cresses, Nasturtium, Purslane,	One whole Lettuce Two parts. Four parts. Two parts. One part.
August,	Green Herbs by themselves, or mingl'd with the Blanch'd.	Lop-Lettuce, Belgrade, or Crum-pen-Lettuce. Tarragon, Sorrel, French, Burnet, Trip-Madame,	Two parts. One part. Two parts of each. One part.
and September.			
October,	Blanch'd	Endive, Sellery,	Two if large, four if small, Stalk and part of the Root and tenderest Leaves.
November.		Lop-Lettuce, Lambs-Lettuce, Radish, Cresses, Turneps,	An handful of each. Three parts. Two parts. One part of each.
and	Green	Mustard Seedlings, Cresses, broad, Spinach,	One part of each. Two parts of each.
December.			

ACETARIA.

A

DISCOURSE

OF

SALLETS.

By *J. E.* S. R. S. Author of
the *Kalendarium.*

Οὐ παντὸς ανδρὸς ἔστιν ἀρτῦσαι καλῶς.
Crat. in Glauc.

LONDON,

Printed for *B. Tooke* at the *Middle-
Temple* Gate in *Fleetstreet,* 1699.

To the
Right Honourable
JOHN
Lord SOMERS
OF
EVESHAM.

Lord High-Chancellor of England, and President of the
Royal-Society.

My Lord,

THE idea and plan of the Royal-Society, having been first conceiv'd and delineated by a great and learned Chancellor, which high office your lordship deservedly bears; not as an acquisition of fortune, but your intellectual endowments; conspicuous (among other excellencies) by the inclination your lordship discovers to promote natural knowledge: as it justifies the discernment of that assembly, to pitch upon your lordship for their president, so does it no less discover the candor, yea, I presume to say, the sublimity of your mind, in so generously honoring them with your acceptance of the choice they have made.

A Chancellor, and a very learned lord, was the first who honoured the chair; and a no less honourable and learned Chancellor, resigns it to your lordship: so as after all the difficulties and hardships the Society has hitherto gone through; it has thro' the favour and protection of its presidents, not only preserv'd its reputation from the malevolence of enemies and detracters, but gone on culminating, and

1

now triumphantly in your lordship: under whose propitious influence, I am perswaded, it may promise itself that, which indeed has hitherto been wanting, to justifie the glorious title it bears of a ROYAL SOCIETY. The emancipating it from some remaining and discouraging circumstances, which it as yet labours under; among which, that of a precarious and unsteady abode, is not the least.

This honor was reserv'd for your lordship; and an honor, permit me to call it, not at all unworthy the owning of the greatest person living: namely, the establishing and promoting real knowledge; and (next to what is divine) truly so called; as far, at least, as humane nature extends towards the knowledge of nature, by enlarging her empire beyond the land of spectres, forms, intentional species, vacuum, occult qualities, and other inadequate notions; which, by their obstreperous and noisy disputes, affrighting, and (till of late) deterring men from adventuring on further discoveries, confin'd them in a lazy acquiescence, and to be fed with fantasms and fruitless speculations, which signifie nothing to the specifick nature of things, solid and useful knowledge; by the investigation of causes, principles, energies, powers, and effects of bodies, and things visible; and to improve them for the good and benefit of mankind.

My lord, that which the Royal Society needs to accomplish an entire freedom, and (by rendring their circumstances more easie) capable to subsist with honor, and to reach indeed the glorious ends of its institution, is an establishment in a more settl'd, appropriate, and commodious place; having hitherto (like the Tabernacle in the wilderness) been only ambulatory for almost forty years: but Solomon built the first temple; and what forbids us to hope, that as great a prince may build Solomon's house, as that great Chancellor (one of your lordship's learned predecessors) had design'd the plan; there being nothing in that august and noble model impossible, or beyond the power of nature and learned industry.

Thus, whilst King Solomon's Temple was consecrated to the god of nature, and his true worship; this may be dedicated, and set apart for the works of nature; deliver'd from those illusions and impostors, that are still endeavouring to cloud and depress the true, and substantial philosophy: a shallow and superficial insight, wherein (as that incomparable person rightly observes) having made so many atheists: whilst a profound, and thorow penetration into her recesses (which is the business of the Royal Society) would lead men to the knowledge, and admiration of the glorious author.

And now, my lord, I expect some will wonder what my meaning is, to usher in a trifle, with so much magnificence, and end at last in a fine receipt for the dressing of a sallet with an handful of pot-herbs! But yet, my lord, this subject, as low and despicable as it appears, challenges a part of natural history; and the greatest princes have thought it no disgrace, not only to make it their diversion, but their care, and to promote and encourage it in the midst of their weightiest affairs: he who wrote of the cedar of Libanus, wrote also of the hysop which grows upon the wall.

To verifie this, how much might I say of gardens and rural employments, preferrable to the pomp and grandeur of other secular business, and that in the estimate of as great men as any age has produc'd! And it is of such great souls we have it recorded; that after they had perform'd the noblest exploits for the publick, they sometimes chang'd their scepters for the spade, and their purple for the gardiner's apron. And of these, some, my lord, were emperors, kings, consuls, dictators, and wise statesmen; who amidst the most important affairs, both in peace and war, have quitted all their pomp and dignity in exchange of this learned pleasure: nor that of the most refin'd part of agriculture (the philosophy of the garden and parterre only) but of herbs, and wholesome sallets, and other plain and useful parts of geoponicks, and wrote books of tillage and husbandry; and took the plough-tackle for their banner, and their names from the grain and pulse they sow'd, as the marks and characters of the highest honor.

But I proceed no farther on a topic so well known to your lordship: nor urge I examples of such illustrious persons laying aside their grandeur, and even of deserting their stations; (which would infinitely prejudice the publick, when worthy men are in place, and at the helm) but to shew how consistent the diversions of the garden and villa were, with the highest and busiest employment of the common-wealth, and never thought a reproch, or the least diminution to the gravity and veneration due to their persons, and the noble rank they held.

Will your lordship give me leave to repeat what is said of the Younger Pliny, (nephew to the naturalist) and whom I think we may parallel with the greatest of his time (and perhaps of any since) under the worthiest Emperor the Roman world ever had? A person of vast abilities, rich, and high in his master's favour; that so husbanded his time, as in the midst of the weightiest affairs, to have answer'd, and by his *example, made good what I have said on this occasion. The ancient and best magistrates of Rome, allow'd but the ninth day for the city and publick business; the rest for the country and the sallet garden: there were then fewer causes indeed at the bar; but never greater justice, nor better judges and advocates. And 'tis hence observed, that we hardly find a great and wise man among the ancients, *qui nullos habuit hortos*, excepting only Pomponius Atticus; whilst his dear Cicero professes, that he never laid out his money

---

*Si quid temporis à civilibus negotiis, quibus totum jam intenderat animum, suffurari potuit, colendis agris, priscos illos Romanos Numam Pompilium, Cincinnatum, Catonem, Fabios, Cicerones, aliosque virtute claros viros imitare; qui in magno honore constituti, vites putare, stercorare agros, & irrigare nequaquam turpe & inhonestum putarunt. In Vit. Plin[y], 2.

more readily, than in the purchasing of gardens, and those sweet retirements, for which he so often left the *rostra* (and court of the greatest and most flourishing state of the world) to visit, prune, and water them with his own hands.

But, my lord, I forget with whom I am talking thus; and a gardiner ought not to be so bold. The present I humbly make your lordship, is indeed but a sallet of crude herbs: but there is among them that which was a prize at the Isthmian games; and your lordship knows who it was both accepted, and rewarded as despicable an oblation of this kind. The favor I humbly beg, is your lordship's pardon for this presumption. The subject is mean, and requires it, and my reputation in danger; should your lordship hence suspect that one could never write so much of dressing sallets, who minded any thing serious, besides the gratifying a sensual appetite with a voluptuary Apician art.

Truly, my lord, I am so far from designing to promote those *supplicia luxuriæ*, (as Seneca calls them) by what I have here written; that were it in my power, I would recall the world, if not altogether to their pristine diet, yet to a much more wholesome and temperate than is now in fashion: and what if they find me like to some who are eager after hunting and other field sports, which are laborious exercises? and fishing, which is indeed a lazy one? who, after all their pains and fatigue, never eat what they take and catch in either: for some such I have known: and tho' I cannot affirm so of my self, (when a well drest and excellent sallet is before me) I am yet a very moderate eater of them. So as to this book-luxury, I can affirm, and that truly what the poet says of himself (on a less innocent occasion) *lasciva pagina, vita proba*. God forbid, that after all I have advanc'd in praise of sallets, I should be thought to plead for the vice I censure, and chuse that of Epicurus for my lemma; *in hac arte consenui*; or to have spent my time in nothing else. The plan annext to these

5

papers, and the apparatus made to superstruct upon it, would acquit me of having bent all my contemplations on sallets only. What I humbly offer your lordship, is (as I said) part of natural history, the product of horticulture, and the field, dignified by the most illustrious, and sometimes tilled *laureato vomere*; which, as it concerns a part of philosophy, I may (without vanity) be allow'd to have taken some pains in cultivating, as an inferior member of the Royal Society.

But, my lord, whilst you read on (if at least you vouchsafe me that honor to read at all) I am conscious I rob the publick of its most precious moments.

I therefore humbly again implore your lordship's pardon: nor indeed needed I to have said half this, to kindle in your breast, that which is already shining there (your lordship's esteem of the Royal Society) after what you were pleas'd to express in such an obliging manner, when it was lately to wait upon your lordship; among whom I had the honor to be a witness of your generous, and favourable acceptance of their addresses, who am,

My Lord,

Your Lordship's

Most Humble and

Most Obedient Servant

JOHN EVELYN.

THE
PREFACE.

T HE favourable entertainment which the *Kalendar* has found,
encouraging the bookseller to adventure upon a ninth
impression, I could not refuse his request of my revising, and giving
it the best improvement I was capable, to an inexhaustible subject,
as it regards a part of horticulture; and offer some little aid to such
as love a diversion so innocent and laudable. There are those of late,
who have arrogated, and given the glorious title of compleat and
accomplish'd gardiners, to what they have publish'd; as if there were
nothing wanting, nothing more remaining, or farther to be expected
from the field; and that nature had been quite emptied of all her fertile
store: whilst those who thus magnifie their discoveries, have after all,
penetrated but a very little way into this vast, ample, and as yet,
unknown territory; who see not, that it would still require the
revolution of many ages; deep, and long experience, for any man to
emerge that perfect, and accomplish'd artist gardiner they boast
themselves to be: nor do I think, men will ever reach the end, and
far extended limits of the vegetable kingdom, so incomprehensible
is the variety it every day produces, of the most useful, and admirable
of all the aspectable works of God; since almost all we see, and touch,
and taste, and smell, eat and drink, are clad with, and defended (from
the greatest prince to the meanest peasant) is furnished from that
great and universal plantation, epitomiz'd in our gardens, highly
worth the contemplation of the most profound divine, and deepest
philosopher.

I should be asham'd to acknowledge how little I have advanc'd, could I find that ever any mortal man from Adam, Noah, Solomon, Aristotle, Theophrastus, Dioscorides, and the rest of nature's interpreters, had ever arriv'd to the perfect knowledge of any one plant, or vulgar weed whatsoever: but this perhaps may yet possibly be reserv'd for another state of things, *and a longer day; that is, when time shall be no more, but knowledge shall be encreas'd.

We have heard of one who studied and contemplated the nature of bees only, for sixty years: after which, you will not wonder, that a person of my acquaintance, should have spent almost forty, in gathering and amassing materials for an hortulan design, to so enormous an heap, as to fill some thousand pages; and yet be comprehended within two, or three acres of ground; nay, within the square of less than one (skilfully planted and cultivated) sufficient to furnish, and entertain his time and thoughts all his life long, with a most innocent, agreeable, and useful employment. But you may justly wonder, and condemn the vanity of it too, with that reproach, this man began to build, but was not able to finish! (Luke 15.30) this has been the fate of that undertaking; and I dare promise, will be of whosoever imagines (without the circumstances of extraordinary assistance, and no ordinary expence) to pursue the plan, erect, and finish the fabrick as it ought to be.

But this is that which abortives the perfection of the most glorious and useful undertakings; the unsatiable coveting to exhaust all that should, or can be said upon every head: if such a one have any thing else to mind, or do in the world, let me tell him, he thinks of building too late; and rarely find we any, who care to superstruct upon the foundation of another, and whose ideas are alike. There ought

---

Ut hujusmodi historiam vix dum incohatum, non ante absolvendam putem, Exitio terras quam dabit una dies. D. Raius [John Ray], *Præfat.* [Preface], *Hist[oria] Plan[tarum]*

therefore to be as many hands, and subsidiaries to such a design (and those masters too) as there are distinct parts of the whole (according to the subsequent table) that those who have the means and courage, may (tho' they do not undertake the whole) finish a part at least, and in time unite their labours into one intire, compleat, and consummate work indeed.

Of one or two of these, I attempted only a specimen in my SILVA and the KALENDAR: imperfect, I say, because they are both capable of great improvements: it is not therefore to be expected. (Let me use the words of an old, and experienc'd gardiner) *Cuncta me dicturum, quæ vastitas ejus scientiæ contineret, sed plurima; nam illud in unius hominis prudentiam cadere non poterit, neque est ulla Disciplina aut Ars, quæ singulari consummata sit ingenio.* (Columella, *de R[e] R[ustica]*, Lib. 5, Cap. 1.)

May it then suffice *aliquam partem tradidisse*, and that I have done my endeavour.

—*Jurtilis olim*

Ne Videar vixisse.

Much more might I add upon this charming, and fruitful subject (I mean, concerning gardening:) but this is not a place to expatiate, deterr'd, as I have long since been, from so bold an enterprize, as the fabrick I mentioned. I content my self then with an humble cottage, and a simple potagere, appendant to the *Calendar*; which, treating only (and that briefly) of the culture of moderate gardens; nothing seems to me, shou'd be more welcome and agreeable, than whilst the product of them is come into more request and use amongst us, than heretofore (beside what we call, and distinguish by the name of fruit) I did annex some particular directions concerning SALLETS.

THE

PLAN

OF A

Royal Garden:

Describing, and Shewing the Amplitude, and Extent of that part of Georgicks, which belongs to Horticulture;

In Three Books.

BOOK I.

BOOK II.

BOOK III.

—Laudato ingentia rura,
Exiguum colito.—

ERRATA.

Page.	Line.	Read
Title, 0	6	εζιν.
Dedicat. 7	8	*Nature*
Præface, 8	penult.	*inutilis*
Plan, *Book* 3 cap.4.		*Gum*
		Commessa
Acetar. 5	10	dele *accept*
6	17	*of which*
16	8	*Halmyridia*
18	20	*are eaten*
26	24	*Sage*
33	11	*Oxelæum*
34	4	*Coss Lettuce*
42	16	*Pig-Nuts*
48	14	dele *Clove,* read *Seeds.*

Page.	Line.	Read
50	12	*resist*
62	15	*Potagere*
74	7	dele *not*
90	5	*Ilanders*
123	14	εζιν
125	17	*Cataclysm*
158	*Marg.*	*Esu sanguinis*
162	13	dele *and*
166	18	*Friers*
183	20	*a well-stor'd*
186	*M.ult.*	*Skirrits*
189	19	*Meaths.*

In the APPENDIX,

RECEITS.

Number 14. *Cucumber. Note,* That the *Cucumbers* and the *Gerkems* are not to be boiled in either of the *Vinegars*; but poured scalding-hot upon them.—And line 7, r. *next day,* or *longer.*

26. *Pudding* of *Carrots. Read thus:* Pare of the Crust and tougher parts of a Two-peny White-Loaf, grating the rest; as also half as much of the Root, a Pint of Fresh Cream, or &c.

In the *Cowslip-Wine* dele *two*; read *ten Gallons.*

[The errata are printed here, with the page and line numbers as in the original. The literals have been corrected in the transcription. The longer amendments to the recipes have not been incorporated into the transcription.]

ACETARIA.

SALLETS in general consist of certain esculent plants and herbs, improv'd by culture, industry, and art of the gard'ner: or, as others say, they are a composition of edule plants and roots of several kinds, to be eaten raw or green, blanch'd or candied; simple, and *per se*, or intermingl'd with others according to the season. The boil'd, bak'd, pickl'd, or otherwise disguis'd, variously accommodated by the skilful cooks, to render them grateful to the more feminine palat, or herbs rather for the pot, &c. challenge not the name of sallet so properly here, tho' sometimes mention'd; and therefore,

Those who criticize not so nicely upon the word, seem to distinguish the *olera (which were never eaten raw) from *acetaria*, which were never boil'd; and so they derive the etymology of *olus,* from *olla*, the pot. But others deduce it from HOLOS [WHOLE], comprehending the universal genus of the vegetable kingdom; as from §PAN [BREAD] *Panis*; esteeming that he who had bread and herbs, was sufficiently bless'd with all a frugal man cou'd need or desire: others again will have it, *ab olendo,* i.e. *crescendo*, from its continual growth and springing up: so the younger Scaliger on Varro: but his father Julius extends it not so generally to all plants, as to all the esculents, according to the text: we call those *olera* (says

---

* *Olera à frigidis* distinct. See Spartianus in *Pescennio*[biography of Pescennius Niger in the *Augustan History*]. Salmas[ius] in *Jul[ius] Capitolin[inus]*.

§   *Panis erat primis virides mortalibus herbæ;*
        Quas tellus nullo follicitante dabat.
   Et modo carpebant vivaci cespite gramen;
        Nunc epulæ tenera fronde cacumen erant.
Ovid, *Fastor. [Fasti],* iv.

*Theophrastus) which are commonly eaten, in which sense it may be taken, to include both boil'd and raw: last of all, *ab alendo*, as having been the original, and genuine food of all mankind from the §Creation.

A great deal more of this learned stuff were to be pick'd up from the *Cumini Sectores*, and impertinently curious; whilst as it concerns the business in hand, we are by sallet to understand a particular composition of certain crude and fresh herbs, such as usually are, or may safely be eaten with some acetous juice, oyl, salt, &c. to give them a grateful gust and vehicle; exclusive of the †PSUCHRAI TRAPEZAI [COLD TABLES], eaten without their due correctives, which the learned #Salmasius, and, indeed generally, the ¶old physicians affirm (and that truly) all crude and raw LACHANA require to render them wholsome; so as probably they were from hence, as ¥Pliny thinks, call'd *acetaria*: and not (as Hermolaus and some others) *acceptaria ab accipiendo;* nor from *accedere*, though so ∞ready at hand, and easily dress'd; requiring neither fire, cost, or attendance, to boil, roast, and prepare them as did flesh and other provisions; from which, and other prerogatives, they were always in use, &c. And hence indeed the more frugal Italians and French, to this day, accept and gather *ogni verdura*, any thing almost that's green and tender, to the very tops of nettles; so as every hedge affords a sallet (not unagreeable) season'd with its proper oxybaphon of vinegar, salt, oyl, &c. which

---

* KALOUMEN GAR LACHANA TA PROS TEN HEMETERAN CHREIAN [FOR WE CALL *LACHANA* (GARDEN HERBS/VEGETABLES) THOSE PLANTS WHICH SERVE OUR NEEDS], Theophrast[us], *[Historia] Plant[arum]*, l[ib]. vii, cap.7.

§ Gen[esis], I, 29.

† Plutarch, *Sympos[iaca]*.

Salmas[ius] in *Solin[us] against Hieron. Mercurialis*.

¶ Galen, *2 R. Aliment*. cap.1, et *Simp. Medic*. Averroes, lib. v. *Colloc. [Colliget]*.

¥ Plin[y], lib. xix, c[ap]. 4.

∞ *Convictus facilis, fine arte, mensa.* Mart[ial], *Ep[igrams]*. 74.

doubtless gives it both the relish and name of salad, *ensalada**, as with us of sallet; from the sapidity, which renders not plants and herbs alone, but men themselves, and their conversations, pleasant and agreeable: but of this enough, and perhaps too much; least whilst I write of salt and sallet, I appear my self insipid: I pass therefore to the ingredients, which we will call

Furniture *and* Materials.

The materials of sallets, which together with the grosser *olera*, consist of roots, stalks, leaves, buds, flowers, &c. Fruits (belonging to another class) would require a much ampler volume, than would suit our *Kalendar*, (to which this pretends to be an appendix only) should we extend the following catalogue further than to a brief enumeration only of such herbaceous plants, *oluscula* and smaller esculents, as are chiefly us'd in cold sallets, of whose culture we have treated there; and as we gather them from the mother and genial bed, with a touch only of their qualities, for reasons hereafter given.

1.   Alexanders, *Hipposelinum*; *S. Smyrnium vulgare* (much of the nature of persly) is moderately hot, and of a cleansing faculty, deobstructing, nourishing, and comforting the stomach. The gentle fresh sprouts, buds and tops are to be chosen, and the stalks eaten in the spring; and when blanch'd, in winter likewise, with oyl, peper, salt, &c. by themselves, or in composition: they make also an excellent vernal pottage.

---

* APURON TROPHEN [FOOD WITHOUT FIRE], which Suidas calls LACHANA. *Olera quæ cruda sumuntur ex Aceto,* Harduin *in loc.*

2.   Artichaux, *Cinara, (Carduus sativus)* hot and dry. The heads being slit in quarters first eaten raw, with oyl, a little vinegar, salt and pepper, gratefully recommend a glass of wine; Dr Muffet says, at the end of meals.

They are likewise, whilst tender and small, fried in fresh butter crisp with persley. But then become a most delicate and excellent restorative, when full grown, they are boil'd the common way. The bottoms are also bak'd in pies, with marrow, dates, and other rich ingredients: in Italy they sometimes broil them, and as the scaly leaves open, baste them with fresh and sweet oyl; but with care extraordinary, for if a drop fall upon the coals, all is marr'd; that hazard escap'd, they eat them with the juice of orange and sugar.

The stalk is blanch'd in autumn, and the pith eaten raw or boil'd. The way of preserving them fresh all winter, is by separating the bottoms from the leaves, and after par-boiling, allowing to every bottom, a small earthen glaz'd pot; burying it all over in fresh melted butter, as they do wild-fowl, &c. Or if more than one, in a larger pot, in the same bed and covering, layer upon layer.

They are also preserv'd by stringing them on pack-thread, a clean paper being put between every bottom, to hinder them from touching one another, and so hung up in a dry place. They are likewise pickl'd.

Tis not very long since this noble thistle came first into Italy, improv'd to this magnitude by culture; and so rare in England, that they were commonly sold for crowns a piece: but what Carthage yearly spent in them (as Pliny computes the sum) amounted to *sestertia sena millia*, 30000 l. sterling.

Note, that the Spanish cardon, a wild and smaller artichoak, with sharp pointed leaves, and lesser head; the stalks being blanch'd and tender, are serv'd-up *a la poiverade* (that is with oyl, pepper, &c.) as the French term is.

3.   Basil, *Ocimum* (as baulm) imparts a grateful flavour, if not too strong, somewhat offensive to the eyes; and therefore the tender tops to be very sparingly us'd in our sallet.

4.   Baulm, *Melissa*, baum, hot and dry, cordial and exhilarating, sovereign for the brain, strengthning the memory, and powerfully chafing away melancholy. The tender leaves are us'd in composition with other herbs; and the sprigs fresh gather'd, put into wine or other drinks, during the heat of summer, give it a marvellous quickness: this noble plant yields an incomparable wine, made as is that of cowslip-flowers.

5.   Beet, *Beta*; of which there is both red, black, and white: the costa, or rib of the white beet (by the French call'd the chard) being boil'd, melts, and eats like marrow. And the roots (especially of the red) cut into thin slices, boil'd, when cold, is of it self a grateful winter sallet; or being mingl'd with other *oluscula*, oyl, vinegar, salt, &c. 'Tis of quality cold and moist, and naturally somewhat laxative: but however by the Epigrammatist stil'd foolish and insipid, as *innocentior quam olus* (for so the learned *Harduin reads the place) 'tis by Diphilus of old, and others since, preferr'd before cabbage as of better nourishment: Martial (not unlearn'd in the art of sallet) commends it with wine and pepper: he names it indeed —*fabrorum prandia*, for its being so vulgar. But eaten with oyl and vinegar, as usually, it is no despicable sallet. There is a beet growing near the sea, which is the most delicate of all. The roots of the red beet, pared into thin slices and circles, are by the French and Italians contriv'd into curious figures to adorn their sallets.

6.   Blite, *Blitum*; English mercury, or (as our country house-wives

---

* Plin[y], *H. Nat.*, lib. xix, cap. 8.

19

call it) all-good, the gentle *turiones*, and tops may be eaten as sparagus, or sodden in pottage: there is both a white and red, much us'd in Spain and Italy; but besides its humidity and detersive nature, 'tis insipid enough.

7. Borrage, *Borrago* (*Gaudia semper ago*) hot and kindly moist, purifying the blood, is an exhilarating cordial, of a pleasant flavour: the tender leaves, and flowers especially, may be eaten in composition; but above all, the sprigs in wine, like those of baum, are of known vertue to revive the hypochondriac, and chear the hard student. See *Bugloss*.

8. Brooklime, *Anagallis aquatica*; moderately hot and moist, prevalent in the scorbute, and stone.

9. Bugloss, *Buglossum;* in nature much like borrage, yet something more astringent. The flowers of both, with the intire plant, greatly restorative, being conserv'd: and for the rest, so much commended by Averroes; that for its effects, cherishing the spirits, justly call'd *euphrosynum*: nay, some will have it the *nepenthes* of Homer: but indeed, what we now call bugloss, was not that of the ancients, but rather borrage, for the like virtue named *Corrago.*

Burnet, see *Pimpinella.*

10. Buds, *Gemmæ, Turiones*; the first rudiments and tops of most sallet-plants, preferrable to all other less tender parts; such as ashen-keys, broom-buds, hot and dry, retaining the vertue of capers, esteem'd to be very opening, and prevalent against the spleen and scurvy; and being pickl'd, are sprinkl'd among the sallets, or eaten by themselves.

11. Cabbage, *Brassica* (and its several kinds) Pompey's beloved

dish, so highly celebrated by old *Cato, Pythagoras, and Chryssippus the Physician (as the only panacea) is not so generally magnify'd by the rest of doctors, as affording but a crass and melancholy juice; yet loosening if but moderately boil'd, if over-much, astringent, according to C. Celsus; and therefore seldom eaten raw, excepting by the Dutch. The cymæ, or sprouts rather of the cole are very delicate, so boil'd as to retain their verdure and green colour. In raising this plant great care is to be had of the seed. The best comes from Denmark and Russia, especially the cauly-flower, (anciently unknown) or from Aleppo. Of the French, the *pancaliere a la large costé*, the white, large and ponderous are to be chosen; and so the cauly-flower: after boiling some steep them in milk, and seethe them again in beef-broth: of old they added a little nitre. The *broccoli* from Naples, perhaps the *halmyridia* of Pliny (or Athenæus rather) *capitata marina & florida*, our sea-keele (the ancient *Crambe*) and growing on our coast, are very delicate, as are the Savoys, commended for being not so rank, but agreeable to most palates, and of better nourishment: in general, cabbages are thought to allay fumes, and prevent intoxication: but some will have them noxious to the sight; others impute it to the cauly-flower rather: but whilst the learned are not agreed about it, Theophrastus affirms the contrary, and Pliny commends the juice raw, with a little honey, for the moist and weeping eye, not the dry or dull. But after all, cabbage ('tis confess'd) is greatly accus'd for lying undigested in the stomach, and provoking eructations; which makes me wonder at the veneration we read the ancients had for them, calling them divine, and swearing, *per brassicam*. 'Tis scarce an hundred years since we first had cabbages out of Holland. Sir Anth. Ashley of Wiburg St. Giles in Dorsetshire, being (as I am told) the first who planted them in England.

---

* *De R[e] R[ustica]*, cap. clvii.

21

12. Cardon, See *Artichaux.*

13. Carrots, *Dauci*, or *Pastinaca sativa*; temperately warm and dry, spicy; the best are yellow, very nourishing; let them be rais'd in ground naturally rich, but not too heavy.

14. Chervile, *Chærophyllum, Myrrhis*; the sweet aromatick Spanish chervile, moderately hot and dry: the tender cimæ, and tops, with other herbs, are never to be wanting in our sallets, (as long as they may be had) being exceedingly wholsome and chearing the spirits: the roots are also boil'd and eaten cold; much commended for aged persons: this (as likewise spinach) is us'd in tarts, and serves alone for divers sauces.

Cibbols.   } *Vide* Onions, *Schœnopræsson*
Cives.

15. Clary, *Horminum*, when tender not to be rejected, and in omlets, made up with cream, fried in sweet butter, are eaten with sugar, juice of orange, or limon.

16. Clavers, *Aparine*; the tender winders, with young nettle-tops, are us'd in Lenten pottages.

17. Corn-sallet, *Valerianella*; loos'ning and refreshing: the tops and leaves are a sallet of themselves, seasonably eaten with other salleting, the whole winter long, and early spring: the French call them *salad de preter*, for their being generally eaten in Lent.

18. Cowslips, *Paralysis*: See *Flowers.*

19. Cresses, *Nasturtium*, garden cresses; to be monthly sown: but above all the Indian, moderately hot, and aromatick, quicken the torpent spirits, and purge the brain, and are of singular effect against the scorbute. Both the tender leaves, calices, capuchin capers, and

flowers, are laudably mixed with the colder plants. The buds being candy'd, are likewise us'd in strewings all winter. There is the *Nastur[tium] Hybernicum* commended also, and the vulgar water-cress, proper in the spring, all of the same nature, tho' of different degrees, and best for raw and cold stomachs, but nourish little.

20.   Cucumber, *Cucumis*; tho' very cold and moist, the most approved sallet alone, or in composition, of all the vinaigrets, to sharpen the appetite, and cool the liver, ¶&c. if rightly prepar'd; that is, by rectifying the vulgar mistake of altogether extracting the juice, in which it should rather be soak'd: nor ought it to be over oyl'd, too much abating of its grateful acidity, and palling the taste, from a contrariety of particles: let them therefore be pared, and cut in thin slices, with a clove or two of onion to correct the crudity, macerated in the juice, often turn'd and moderately drain'd. Others prepare them, by shaking the slices between two dishes, and dress them with very little oyl, well beaten, and mingled with the juice of limon, orange, or vinegar, salt and pepper. Some again, (and indeed the most approv'd) eat them as soon as they are cut, retaining their liquor, which being exhausted (by the former method) have nothing remaining in them to help the concoction. Of old they *boil'd the cucumber, and paring off the rind, eat them with oyl, vinegar, and honey; sugar not being so well known. Lastly, the pulp in broth is greatly refreshing, and may be mingl'd in most sallets, without the least damage, contrary to the common opinion; it not being long, since cucumber, however dress'd, was thought fit to be thrown away, being accounted little better than poyson. Tavernier tells us, that in the Levant, if a child cry for something to eat, they give it a raw cucumber instead of bread. The young ones may be boil'd in white wine. The smaller sort (known by the

¶ EPHTHOS,DOSIKNOS, APALOS, ALOUSTOS, OURETIKOS, Athen[æus].
* *Cucumis elixus delicatior, innocentior.* Athenæus.

name of gerckems) muriated with the seeds of dill, and the mango pickle are for the winter.

21. Daisy, *Buphthalmum*, ox-eye, or *Bellis-major*: The young roots are frequently eaten by the Spaniards and Italians all the spring till June.

22. Dandelion, *Dens Leonis, Condrilla*: Macerated in several waters, to extract the bitterness; tho' somewhat opening, is very wholsome, and little inferior to succory, endive, &c. The French country-people eat the roots; and 'twas with this homely sallet, the good-wife Hecate entertain'd Theseus. See *Sowthistle*.

23. Dock, *Oxylapathum*, or sharp pointed dock: emollient, and tho' otherwise not for our sallet, the roots brewed in ale or beer, are excellent for the scorbute.

Earth-nuts, *Bulbo-castanum*; (found in divers places of Surry, near Kingston, and other parts) the rind par'd off, are eaten crude by rustics, with a little pepper; but are best boil'd like other roots, or in pottage rather, and are sweet and nourishing.

24. Elder, *Sambucus*; The flowers infus'd in vinegar, grateful both to the stomach and taste; attenuate thick and viscid humours; and tho' the leaves are somewhat rank of smell, and so not commendable in sallet; they are otherwise (as indeed is the intire shrub) of the most sovereign vertue; and the spring buds and tender leaves, excellently wholsome in pottage at that season of the year. See *Flowers*.

25. Endive, *Endivium, Intubum sativum*; the largest, whitest, and tenderest leaves best boil'd, and less crude. It is naturally cold, profitable for hot stomachs; incisive and opening obstructions of the liver: the curled is more delicate, being eaten alone, or in composition, with the usual *intinctus*: it is also excellent being boil'd; the middle part

of the blanch'd-stalk separated, eats firm, and the ampler leaves by many preferr'd before lettuce. See *Succory*.

Eschalot. See *Onions*.

26.   Fennel, *Fœniculum*: The sweetest of Bolognia: aromatick, hot, and dry; expels wind, sharpens the sight, and recreates the brain; especially the tender *umbella* and seed-pods. The stalks are to be peel'd when young, and then dress'd like sellery. The tender tufts and leaves emerging, being minc'd, are eaten alone with vinegar, or oyl, and pepper, and to correct the colder materials, enter properly into composition. The Italians eat the blanch'd stalk (which they call *cartucci*) all winter long. There is a very small green-worm, which sometimes lodges in the stemm of this plant, which is to be taken out, as the red one in that of sellery.

27.   Flowers, *Flores*; chiefly of the aromatick esculents and plants are preferrable, as generally endow'd with the vertues of their simples, in a more intense degree; and may therefore be eaten alone in their proper vehicles, or composition with other salleting, sprinkl'd among them; but give a more palatable relish, being infus'd in vinegar; especially those of the clove-gillyflower, elder, orange, cowslip, rosemary, arch-angel, sage, *nasturtium indicum,* &c. Some of them are pickl'd and divers of them make also very pleasant and wholsome theas, as do likewise the wild time, bugloss, mint, &c.

28.   Garlick, *Allium*; dry towards excess; and tho' both by Spaniards and Italians, and the more southern people, familiarly eaten, with almost every thing, and esteem'd of such singular vertue to help concoction, and thought a charm against all infection and poyson (by which it has obtain'd the name of the country man's theriacle) we yet think it more proper for our northern rustics, especially living in uliginous and moist places, or such as use the sea:

whilst we absolutely forbid it entrance into our salleting, by reason of its intolerable rankness, and which made it so detested of old; that the eating of it was (as we read) part of the punishment for such as had committed the horrid'st crimes. To be sure, 'tis not for ladies palats, nor those who court them, farther than to permit a light touch on the dish, with a clove thereof, much better supply'd by the gentler roccombo.

Note, that in Spain they sometimes eat it boil'd, which taming its fierceness, turns it into nourishment, or rather medicine.

Ginny-pepper, *Capsicum.* See *Pepper.*

29. Goats-beard, *Trago-pogon:* The root is excellent even in sallet, and very nutritive, exceeding profitable for the breast, and may be stew'd and dress'd as scorzonera.

30. Hops, *Lupulus*: Hot and moist, rather medicinal, than fit for sallet; the buds and young tendrels excepted, which may be eaten raw; but more conveniently being boil'd, and cold like asparagus: they are diuretic; depurate the blood, and open obstructions.

31. Hyssop, *Hyssopus; Thymus capitatus creticus*; majoran, mary-gold, &c. as all hot, spicy aromatics, (commonly growing in kitchin-gardens) are of faculty to comfort, and strengthen; prevalent against melancholy and phlegm: plants, like these, going under the names of pot-herbs, are much more proper for broths and decoctions, than the tender sallet: yet the tops and flowers reduc'd to powder, are by some reserv'd for strewings, upon the colder ingredients; communicating no ungrateful fragrancy.

32. Jack-by-the-hedge, *Alliaria*, or sauce-alone; has many medicinal properties, and is eaten as other sallets, especially by country people, growing wild under their banks and hedges.

33.　Leeks, and cibbols, *Porrum*; hot, and of vertue prolifick; since Latona, the mother of Apollo long'd after them: the Welch, who eat them much, are observ'd to be very fruitful: they are also friendly to the lungs and stomach, being sod in milk; a few therefore of the slender and green summities, a little shred, do not amiss in composition. See *Onion*.

34.　Lettuce, *Lactuca*: Tho' by metaphor call'd *mortuorum cibi*, (to say nothing of §Adonis and his sad mistriss) by reason of its soporiferous quality, ever was, and still continues the principal foundation of the universal tribe of sallets; which is to cool and refresh, besides its other properties: and therefore in such high esteem with the ancients; that divers of the Valerian family, dignify'd and enobled their name with that of *Lactucinii*.

It is indeed of nature more cold and moist than any of the rest; yet less astringent, and so harmless that it may safely be eaten raw in fevers; for it allays heat, bridles choler, extinguishes thirst, excites appetite, kindly nourishes, and above all represses vapours, conciliates sleep, mitigates pain; besides the effect it has upon the morals, temperance and chastity. Galen (whose beloved sallet it was) from its pinguid, subdulcid and agreeable nature, says it breeds the most laudable blood. No marvel then that they were by the ancients called *sana*, by way of eminency, and so highly valu'd by the great ¶Augustus, that attributing his recovery of a dangerous sickness to them, 'tis reported, he erected a statue, and built an altar to this noble plant. And that the most abstemious and excellent Emperor †Tacitus

---

* Eubulus.

§ *In lactuca occultatum à Venere Adonin cecinit Callimachus, quod Allegoricè interpretatus Athenæus illuc referendum putat quod in Venerem hebetiores fiant lactucis vescentes assiduè.*

¶ *Apud* Sueton[ius].

† Vopiscus, *Tacit[us]*. For the rest both of the kinds and vertues of lettuce, see Plin[y], *H[istoria] N[aturalis]*, l[ib]. xix., c[ap]. 8 and xx, c. 7. Fernel, &c.

(spending almost nothing at his frugal table in other dainties) was yet so great a friend to lettuce, that he was us'd to say of his prodigality, *somnum se mercari illa sumptus effusione.* How it was celebrated by Galen we have heard; how he us'd it he tells himself; namely, beginning with lettuce in his younger days, and concluding with it when he grew old, and that to his great advantage. In a word, we meet with nothing among all our crude materials and sallet store, so proper to mingle with any of the rest, nor so wholsome to be eaten alone, or in composition, moderately, and with the usual oxelæum of vinegar, pepper, and oyl, &c. which last does not so perfectly agree with the alphange, to which the juice of orange, or limon and sugar is more desirable: Aristoxenus is reported to have irrigated his lettuce-beds with an oinomelite, or mixture of wine and honey: and certainly 'tis not for nothing that our garden-lovers, and brothers of the sallet, have been so exceedingly industrious to cultivate this noble plant, and multiply its species; for to name a few in present use: we have the alphange of Montpelier, crisp and delicate; the Arabic; ambervelleres; Belgrade, cabbage, capuchin, coss-lettuce, curl'd; the Genoa (lasting all the winter) the imperial, lambs, or agnine, and lobbs or lop-lettuces. The French minion a dwarf kind: the oak-leaf, passion, Roman, shell, and Silesian, hard and crimp (esteemed of the best and rarest) with divers more: and here let it be noted, that besides three or four sorts of this plant, and some few of the rest, there was within our remembrance, rarely any other salleting serv'd up to the best tables; with unblanch'd endive, succory, purselan, (and indeed little other variety) sugar and vinegar being the constant vehicles (without oyl) but now sugar is almost wholly banish'd from all, except the more effeminate palates, as too much palling, and taking from the grateful acid now in use, tho' otherwise not totally to be reproved: lettuce boil'd and condited is sometimes spoken of.

35.   Limon, *Limonia, citrea mala;* exceedingly refreshing, cordial, &c. The pulp being blended with the juice, secluding the over-sweet or bitter. See *Orange.*

36.   Mallow, *Malva*; the curl'd, emollient, and friendly to the ventricle, and so rather medicinal; yet may the tops, well boil'd, be admitted, and the rest (tho' out of use at present) was taken by the poets for all sallets in general. Pythagoras held *malvæ folium sanctissimum*; and we find Epimenides in *Plato at his mallows and asphodel; and indeed it was of old the first dish at table: the Romans had it also *in deliciis,* ¶*malvæ salubres corpori*, approved by §Galen and #Dioscorides; namely the garden-mallow, by others the wild; but I think both proper rather for the pot, than sallet. Nonius supposes the tall *rosea*, arborescent holi-hocks that bears the broad flower, for the best, and very ¥laxative; but by reason of their clamminess and lentor, banished from our sallet, tho' by some commended and eaten with oyl and vinegar, and some with butter.

Mercury, *Bonus Henricus*, English mercury, or *Lapathum unctuosum*. See *Blitum.*

37.   Melon, *Melo*; to have been reckon'd rather among fruits; and tho' an usual ingredient in our sallet; yet for its transcendent delicacy and flavor, cooling and exhilarating nature (if sweet, dry, weighty,

---

* *De Legib[us].*
¶ Hor[ace], *Epod[es]*, II.
§ *De Simp. Medic.*, L[ib]. vii.
# Lib. ii, cap. 3.
¥ *Exoneraturas ventrem mihi villica malvas*
  Attulit, & varias, quas habet hortus, opes. Mart[ial], Lib. x.
  And our sweet poet:
          —*Nulla est humanior herba,*
      Nulla magis suavi commoditate bona est,
      Omnia tam placidè regerat, blandéque relaxat,
      Emollítque vias, nec sinit esse rudes. Cow[ley], *Plan[tarum]*, L[ib]. 4.

and well-fed) not only superior to all the gourd-kind, but paragon with the noblest productions of the garden. Jos. Scaliger and Casaubon, think our melon unknown to the ancients, (which others contradict) as yet under the name of cucumers: but he who reads how artificially they were cultivated, rais'd under glasses, and expos'd to the hot sun, (for Tiberius) cannot well doubt of their being the same with ours.

There is also a winter-melon, large and with black seeds, exceedingly cooling, brought us from abroad, and the hotter climates, where they drink water after eating melons; but in the colder (after all dispute) wine is judg'd the better: that it has indeed by some been accus'd as apt to corrupt in the stomach (as do all things else eaten in excess) is not deny'd: but a perfect good melon is certainly as harmless a fruit as any whatsoever; and may safely be mingl'd with sallet, in pulp or slices, or more properly eaten by it self, with a little salt and pepper; for a melon which requires sugar to commend it, wants of perfection. *Note*, that this fruit was very rarely cultivated in England, so as to bring it to maturity, till Sir Geo. Gardner came out of Spain. I my self remembring, when an ordinary melon would have been sold for five or six shillings. The small unripe fruit, when the others are past, may be pickl'd with mango, and are very delicate.

38.   Mint, *Mentha*; the *Angustifolia spicata*, spear-mint; dry and warm, very fragrant, a little press'd, is friendly to the weak stomach, and powerful against all nervous crudities: the gentler tops of the orange-mint, enter well into our composition, or are grateful alone (as are also the other sorts) with the juice of orange, and a little sugar.

39.   Mushroms, *Fungi*; by the *Orator call'd *terræ*, by Porphyry *deorum filii*, without seed (as produc'd by the midwifry of autumnal

---

* Cic[ero], *[Epistulae] ad Attic[um]*.

thunder-storms, portending the mischief they cause) by the French, *champignons*, with all the species of the *boletus*, &c. for being, as some hold, neither root, herb, flower, nor fruit, nor to be eaten crude; should be therefore banish'd entry into our sallet, were I to order the composition; however so highly contended for by many, as the very principal and top of all the rest; whilst I think them tolerable only (at least in this climate) if being fresh and skilfully chosen, they are accommodated with the nicest care and circumspection; generally reported to have something malignant and noxious in them: nor without cause; from the many sad examples, frequent mischiefs, and funest accidents they have produc'd, not only to particular persons, but whole families: exalted indeed they were to the second course of the Cæsarian tables, with the noble title BROMA THEON [FOOD OF THE GODS], a dainty fit for the gods alone; to whom they sent the Emperor ¶Claudius, as they have many since, to the other world. But he that reads how Seneca§ deplores his lost friend, that brave commander Annæus Serenus, and several other gallant persons with him, who all of them perish'd at the same repast; would be apt to ask with the #Naturalist (speaking of this suspicious dainty) *que voluptas tanta ancipitis cibi*? and who indeed would hazard it? So true is that of the poet; he that eats mushroms, many times *Nil amplius edit*, eats no more perhaps all his life after. What other deterring epithets are given for our caution, BARE PNIGOENTA MUKETON [THE CHOKING WEIGHTS OF MUSHROOMS], heavy and choaking. (Athenæus reporting of the poet Euripides's, finding a woman and her three children strangl'd by eating of them) one would think sufficient warning.

Among these comes in the *Fungus reticularis,* to be found about London, as at Fulham and other places; whilst at no small charge we

¶ Sueton[ius], in *Claudi[us]*.
§ Sen[eca], *[Epistulae]*, lxiii.
# Plin[y], *N[aturalis] H[istoria]*, l[ib].xxi , c[ap]. 23.

send for them into France; as we also do for trufles, pig-nuts, and other subterraneous tubera, which in Italy they fry in oyl, and eat with pepper: they are commonly discovered by a nasute swine purposely brought up; being of a chessnut colour, and heady smell, and not seldom found in England, particularly in a park of my Lord Cotton's, at Rushton or Rusbery in Northampton-shire, and doubtless in other *places too were they sought after. How these rank and provocative excrescences are to be ¶treated (of themselves insipid enough, and only famous for their kindly taking any pickle or conditure) that they may do the less mischief, we might here set down. But since there be so many ways of dressing them, that I can incourage none to use them, for reasons given (besides that they do not at all concern our safer and innocent sallet furniture) I forbear it; and referr those who long after this beloved ragout, and other *voluptuaria venena* (as Seneca calls them) to what our learned Dr. Lyster§ says of the many venomous insects harbouring and corrupting in a new found-out species of mushroms had lately *in deliciis*. Those in the mean time, which are esteemed best, and less pernicious, (of which see the Appendix) are such as rise in rich, airy, and dry #pasture-grounds; growing on the staff or pedicule of about an inch thick and high; moderately swelling (target-like) round and firm, being underneath of a pale saffronish hue, curiously radiated in parallel lines and edges, which becoming either yellow, orange, or black, are to be rejected: but besides what the harvest-months produce, they are likewise rais'd

---

* *Transact. Philos.* [*Philosophical Transactions of the Royal Society*], num. 202. [Evelyn refers to Rushton Hall, Northamptonshire, the property of the Cokayne family, the Viscounts Cullen.]

¶ Apitius [Apicius], lib. vii, cap. 13.

§ *Philos[ophical] Transact[ions]*, Num. 89, 'Journey to Paris'.

Pratensibus optima fungis Natura est: aliis male creditur, Hor[ace], *Sat[ires]*, l[ib]. 7, Sat. 4.

¶artificially; as at Naples in their wine-cellars, upon an heap of rank earth, heaped upon a certain supposed stone, but in truth, (as the curious and noble *Peiresky tells us, he found to be) nothing but an heap of old fungus's, reduc'd and compacted to a stony hardness, upon which they lay earth, and sprinkle it with warm water, in which mushroms have been steeped. And in France, by making an hot bed of asses-dung, and when the heat is in temper, watering it (as above) well impregnated with the parings and offals of refuse fungus's; and such a bed will last two or three years, and sometimes our common melon-beds afford them, besides other experiments.

40.   Mustard, *Sinapi;* exceeding hot and mordicant, not only in the seed but leaf also; especially in seedling young plants, like those of radishes (newly peeping out of the bed) is of incomparable effect to quicken and revive the spirits; strengthening the memory, expelling heaviness, preventing the vertiginous palsie, and is a laudable cephalick. Besides it is an approv'd antiscorbutick; aids concoction, cuts and dissipates phlegmatick humours. In short, 'tis the most noble embamma, and so necessary an ingredient to all cold and raw salleting, that it is very rarely, if at all, to be left out. In Italy in making mustard, they mingle limon and orange-peel, with the seeds. How the best is made, see hereafter.

Nasturtium Indicum. See *Cresses.*

41.   Nettles, *Urtica*; hot, dry, diuretic, solvent; purifies the blood: the buds, and very tender cimæ, a little bruised, are by some eaten raw, by others boil'd, especially in spring-pottage, with other herbs.

¶ Bacon, *Nat. Hist. [History Naturall and Experimentall of Life and Death]*, 12. Cent. vii. 547, 548, &c.
* Gassend[i], *Vita Peir[e]s[ky]*, l[ib]. iv. Raderus Mart[ial], l[ib]. [–], Epigram xlvi, *In Ponticum*, says, within four days.

42.   Onion, *Cepa, Porrum*; the best are such as are brought us out of Spain, whence they of St. Omers had them, and some that have weigh'd eight pounds. Choose therefore the large, round, white, and thin skin'd. Being eaten crude and alone with oyl, vinegar, and pepper, we own them in sallet, not so hot as garlick, nor at all so rank: boil'd, they give a kindly relish; raise appetite, corroborate the stomach, cut phlegm, and profit the asthmatical: but eaten in excess, are said to offend the head and eyes, unless edulcorated with a gentle maceration. In the mean time, as to their being noxious to the sight, is imputable only to the vapour rising from the raw onion, when peeled, which some commend for its purging and quickning that sense. How they are us'd in pottage, boil'd in milk, stew'd, &c. concerns the kitchin. In our cold sallet we supply them with the *porrum sectile*, tops of leeks, and eschalots (*Ascalonia*) of gust more exalted, yet not to the degree of garlick. Or (by what of later use is much preferr'd) with a clove or two of raccombo, of a yet milder and delicate nature, which by rubbing the dish only, imparts its vertue agreeably enough. In Italy they frequently make a sallet of scalions, cives, and chibbols only season'd with oyl and pepper; and an honest laborious countryman, with good bread, salt, and a little parsley, will make a contented meal with a roasted onion. How this noble bulb was deified in *Egypt we are told, and that whilst they were building the pyramids, there was spent in this root ¶ninety tun of gold among the workmen. So lushious and tempting it seems they were, that as whole nations have subsisted on them alone; so the Israelites were ready to return to slavery and brick-making for the love of them. Indeed Hecamedes we find presents them to Patroclus, in Homer, as a regalo; but certainly we are either mistaken in the species (which some will have to be melons) or use poetick licence, when we so highly magnify them.

---

* *O Sanctas gentes, quibus hæc nascuntur in hortis Numina.* Juv[enal], *Sat[ire]* 15.
¶ Herodotus.

43.   Orach, *Atriplex*: Is cooling, allays the pituit humor: being set over the fire, neither this, nor lettuce, needs any other water than their own moisture to boil them in, without expression: the tender leaves are mingl'd with other cold salleting; but 'tis better in pottage. See *Blitum*.

44.   Orange, *Arantiæ* (*Malum aureum*) moderately dry, cooling, and incisive; sharpens appetite, exceedingly refreshes and resists putrefaction: we speak of the sub acid; the sweet and bitter orange being of no use in our sallet. The limon is somewhat more acute, cooling and extinguishing thirst; of all the OXUBAPHA [VINEGAR DIPPERS/DISHES] the best *succedaneum* to vinegar. The very spoils and rinds of orange and limon being shred and sprinkl'd among the other herbs, correct the acrimony. But they are tender seedlings from the hot-bed, which impart an aromatic exceedingly grateful to the stomach. Vide *Limon*.

45.   Parsnep, *Pastinaca*, carrot; first boil'd, being cold, is of it self a winter-sallet, eaten with oyl, vinegar, &c. and having something of spicy, is by some, thought more nourishing than the turnep.

46.   Pease, *Pisum*; the pod of the sugar-pease, when first beginning to appear, with the husk and tendrels, affording a pretty acid, enter into the composition, as do those of hops and the vine.

47.   Peper, *Piper*; hot and dry in a high degree; of approv'd vertue against all flatulency proceeding from cold and phlegmatic constitutions, and generally all crudities whatsoever; and therefore for being of universal use to correct and temper the cooler herbs, and such as abound in moisture; it is a never to be omitted ingredient of our sallets; provided it be not too minutely beaten (as oft we find it) to an almost impalpable dust, which is very pernicious, and frequently adheres and sticks in the folds of the stomach, where,

instead of promoting concoction, it often causes a cardialgium, and fires the blood: it should therefore be grosly contus'd only.

Indian capsicum, superlatively hot and burning, is yet by the Africans eaten with salt and vinegar by it self, as an usual condiment; but wou'd be of dangerous consequence with us; being so much more of an acrimonious and terribly biting quality, which by art and mixture is notwithstanding render'd not only safe, but very agreeable in our sallet. Take the pods, and dry them well in a pan; and when they are become sufficiently hard, cut them into small pieces, and stamp 'em in a mortar to dust: to each ounce of which add a pound of wheat-flour, fermented with a little *levain*: kneed and make them into cakes or loaves cut long-wise, in shape of Naples-biscuit. These re-bake a second time, till they are stone-hard: pound them again as before, and serce it through a fine sieve, for a very proper seasoning, instead of vulgar peper. The mordicancy thus allay'd, be sure to make the mortar very clean, after having beaten Indian capsicum, before you stamp any thing in it else. The green husks, or first peeping buds of the walnut-tree, dry'd to powder, serve for peper in some places, and so do myrtle berries.

48.   Parsley, *Petroselinum*, or *Apium hortense*; being hot and dry, opens obstructions, is very diuretic, yet nourishing, edulcorated in shifted warm water (the roots especially) but of less vertue than alexanders; nor so convenient in our crude sallet, as when decocted on a medicinal account. Some few tops of the tender leaves may yet be admitted; tho' it was of old, we read, never brought to the table at all, as sacred to oblivium and the defunct. In the mean time, there being nothing more proper for stuffing, (*farces*) and other sauces, we consign it to the olitories. Note, that persley is not so hurtful to the eyes as is reported. See *Sellery*.

49.   Pimpernel, *Pimpinella*; eaten by the French and Italians, is our

common burnet; of so chearing and exhilarating a quality, and so generally commended, as (giving it admittance into all sallets) 'tis pass'd into a proverb:

> *L'Insalata non è buon, ne bella,*
> *Ove non è la pimpinella.*

But a fresh sprig in wine, recommends it to us as its most genuine element.

50.   Purslain, *Portulaca*; especially the golden whilst tender next the seed-leaves, with the young stalks, being eminently moist and cooling, quickens appetite, asswages thirst, and is very profitable for hot and bilious tempers, as well as sanguine, and generally entertain'd in all our sallets, mingled with the hotter herbs: 'tis likewise familiarly eaten alone with oyl and vinegar; but with moderation, as having been sometimes found to corrupt in the stomach, which being pickl'd 'tis not so apt to do. Some eat it cold, after it has been boil'd, which Dr. Muffet would have in wine, for nourishment.

The shrub *halimus*, is a sort of sea-purslain: the newly peeping leaves (tho' rarely us'd) afford a not unpleasant *acidulæ*, even during winter, if it prove not too severe.

Purslain is accus'd for being hurtful to the teeth, if too much eaten.

51.   Radish, *Raphanus*. Albeit rather medicinal, than so commendably accompanying our sallets (wherein they often slice the larger roots) are much inferior to the young seedling leaves and roots; raised on the *monthly hot-bed, almost the whole year round, affording a very grateful mordacity, and sufficiently attempers the cooler ingredients: the bigger roots (so much desir'd) should be such as being transparent, eat short and quick, without stringiness, and not

---

* PROS TO RADIOS PHAINESTHAI [SO THAT THEY MAY APPEAR EASILY], *quia tertio à fatu die appareat.*

too biting. These are eaten alone with salt only, as carrying their peper in them; and were indeed by Dioscorides and Pliny celebrated above all roots whatsoever; insomuch as in the Delphic temple, there was *raphanus ex auro dicatus*, a radish of solid gold; and 'tis said of Moschius, that he wrote a whole volume in their praise. Notwithstanding all which, I am sure, the great ¶Hippocrates utterly condemns them, as *vitiosæ, innatantes ac ægre concoctiles*. And the Naturalist calls it *cibus illiberalis*, fitter for rustics than gentlemens tables. And indeed (besides that they decay the teeth) experience tells us, that as the Prince of Physicians writes, it is hard of digestion, inimicous to the stomach, causing nauseous eructations, and sometimes vomiting, tho' otherwise diuretic, and thought to repel vapours of wine, when the wits were at their genial club. Dioscorides and #Galen differ about their eating; one prescribes it before meals, the latter for after. Some macerate the young roots in warm milk, to render them more nourishing.

There is a *raphanus rusticanus*, the Spanish black horse-radish, of a hotter quality, and not so friendly to the head; but a notable antiscorbutic, which may be eaten all the winter, and on that account an excellent ingredient in the composition of mustard; as are also the thin shavings, mingled with our cold herbs. And now before I have done with this root, for an excellent and universal condiment. Take horse-radish, whilst newly drawn out of the earth, otherwise laid to steep in water a competent time; then grate it on a grater which has no bottom, that so it may pass thro', like a mucilage, into a dish of earthen ware: this temper'd with vinegar, in which a little sugar has been dissolv'd, you have a sauce supplying mustard to the sallet, and serving likewise for any dish besides.

¶ *De diæta*, Lib. ii, cap. 25.
# *De Aliment. Facult.*, Lib. ii.

52.   Rampion, *Rapunculus*, or the esculent campanula: the tender roots eaten in the spring, like those of radishes, but much more nourishing.

53.   Rocket, *Eruca* Spanish; hot and dry, to be qualified with lettuce, purcelain, and the rest, &c. See *Tarragon*.

Roccombo. See *Onions*.

54.   Rosemary, *Rosmarinus*; soverainly cephalic, and for the memory, sight, and nerves, incomparable: and tho' not us'd in the leaf with our sallet furniture, yet the flowers, a little bitter, are always welcome in vinegar; but above all, a fresh sprig or two in a glass of wine. See *Flowers*.

55.   Sage, *Salvia*; hot and dry. The tops of the red, well pick'd and wash'd (being often defil'd with venomous slime, and almost imperceptible insects) with the flowers, retain all the noble properties of the other hot plants; more especially for the head, memory, eyes, and all paralytical affections. In short, 'tis a plant endu'd with so many and wonderful properties, as that the assiduous use of it is said to render men immortal: we cannot therefore but allow the tender summities of the young leaves; but principally the flowers in our cold sallet; yet so as not to domineer.

Salsifax, *Scorzonera*. See *Vipergrass*.

56.   Sampier, *Crithmum*: That growing on the sea-cliffs (as about Dover, &c.) not only pickl'd, but crude and cold, when young and tender (and such as we may cultivate, and have in our kitchin-gardens, almost the year round) is in my opinion, for its aromatic, and other excellent vertues and effects against the spleen, cleansing the passages, sharpening appetite, &c. so far preferrable to most of

our hotter herbs, and sallet-ingredients, that I have long wonder'd, it has not been long since propagated in the potagere, as it is in France; from whence I have often receiv'd the seeds, which have prosper'd better, and more kindly with me, that what comes from our own coasts: it does not indeed pickle so well, as being of a more tender stalk and leaf: but in all other respects for composing sallets, it has nothing like it.

57.   Scalions, *Ascalonia, Cepæ*; the French call them *appetites*, which it notably quickens and stirs up: corrects crudities, and promotes concoction. The Italians steep them in water, mince, and eat them cold with oyl, vinegar, salt, &c.

58.   Scurvy-grass, *Cochlearia*, of the garden, but especially that of the sea, is sharp, biting, and hot; of nature like nasturtium, prevalent in the scorbute. A few of the tender leaves may be admitted in our composition. See *Nasturtium Indicum*.

59.   Sellery, *Apium Italicum*, (and of the *Petroseline* family) was formerly a stranger with us (not very long since in Italy) is an hot and more generous sort of Macedonian persley, or smallage. The tender leaves of the blancht stalk do well in our sallet, as likewise the slices of the whiten'd stems, which being crimp and short, first peel'd and slit longwise, are eaten with oyl, vinegar, salt and peper; and for its high and grateful taste, is ever plac'd in the middle of the grand sallet, at our great mens tables, and prætors feasts, as the grace of the whole board. Caution is to be given of a small red worm, often lurking in these stalks, as does the green in fennil.

Shallots. See *Onion*.

60.   Skirrets, *Sisarum*; hot and moist, corroborating, and good for the stomach, exceedingly nourishing, wholsome and delicate; of all

the root-kind, not subject to be windy, and so valued by the Emperor Tiberius, that he accepted them for tribute.

This excellent root is seldom eaten raw; but being boil'd, stew'd, roasted under the embers, bak'd in pies, whole, sliced, or in pulp, is very acceptable to all palates. 'Tis reported they were heretofore something bitter; see what culture and education effects!

61.   Sorrel, *Acetosa:* of which there are divers kinds. The French *acetocella*, with the round leaf, growing plentifully in the north of England; Roman *oxalis*; the broad German, &c. but the best is of Green-land: by nature cold, abstersive, acid, sharpning appetite, asswages heat, cools the liver, strengthens the heart; is an anti-scorbutic, resisting putrefaction, and imparting so grateful a quickness to the rest, as supplies the want of orange, limon, and other omphacia, and therefore never to be excluded. Vide *Wood-sorrel.*

62.   Sow-thistle, *Sonchus;* of the intybus-kind. Galen was us'd to eat it as lettuce; exceedingly welcome to the late Morocco Ambass–ador and his retinue.

63.   Sparagus, *Asparagus (ab Asperitate)* temperately hot, and moist; cordial, diuretic, easie of digestion, and next to flesh, nothing more nourishing, as Sim. Sethius, an excellent physician holds. They are sometimes, but very seldom, eaten raw with oyl, and vinegar; but with more delicacy (the bitterness first exhausted) being so speedily boil'd, as not to lose the verdure and agreeable tenderness; which is done by letting the water boil, before you put them in. I do not esteem the Dutch greater and larger sort (especially rais'd by the rankness of the beds) so sweet and agreeable, as those of a moderate size.

64.   Spinach, *Spinachia:* of old not us'd in sallets, and the oftner kept out the better; I speak of the crude: but being boil'd to a pult, and without other water than its own moisture, is a most excellent

condiment with butter, vinegar, or limon, for almost all sorts of boil'd flesh, and may accompany a sick man's diet. 'Tis laxative and emollient, and therefore profitable for the aged, and (tho' by original a Spaniard) may be had at almost any season, and in all places.

Stone-crop, *Sedum minus*. See *Trick-madame*.

65.   Succory, *Cichorium*, an intube; erratic and wild, with a narrow dark leaf, different from the sative, tho' probably by culture only; and for being very bitter, a little edulcorated with sugar and vinegar, is by some eaten in the summer, and more grateful to the stomach than the palate. See *Endive*.

66.   Tansy, *Tanacetum*; hot and cleansing; but in regard of its domineering relish, sparingly mixt with our cold sallet, and much fitter (tho' in very small quantity) for the pan, being qualified with the juices of other fresh herbs, spinach, green corn, violet, primrose-leaves, &c. at entrance of the spring, and then fried brownish, is eaten hot with the juice of orange and sugar, as one of the most agreeable of all the boil'd herbaceous dishes.

67.   Tarragon, *Draco herba*, of Spanish extraction; hot and spicy: the tops and young shoots, like those of rochet, never to be secluded our composition, especially where there is much lettuce. 'Tis highly cordial and friendly to the head, heart, liver, correcting the weakness of the ventricle, etc.

68.   Thistle, *Carduus mariæ*; our lady's milky or dappl'd thistle, disarm'd of its prickles, is worth esteem: the young stalk about May, being peel'd and soak'd in water, to extract the bitterness, boil'd or raw, is a very wholsome sallet, eaten with oyl, salt, and peper: some eat them sodden in proper broth, or bak'd in pies, like the artichoak; but the tender stalk boil'd or fry'd, some preferr; both nourishing and restorative.

69.   Trick-madame, *Sedum minus*, stone-crop; is cooling and moist, grateful to the stomach. The cimata and tops, when young and tender, dress'd as purselane, is a frequent Ingredient in our cold sallet.

70.   Turnep, *Rapum*; moderately hot and moist: *Napus*; the long *Navet* is certainly the most delicate of them, and best nourishing. Pliny speaks of no fewer than six sorts, and of several colours; some of which were suspected to be artificially tinged. But with us, the yellow is preferr'd; by others the red Bohemian. But of whatever kind, being sown upon the hot-bed, and no bigger than seedling radish, they do excellently in composition; as do also the stalks of the common turnep, when first beginning to bud.

And here should not be forgotten, that wholsome, as well as agreeable sort of bread, we are *taught to make; and of which we have eaten at the greatest persons tables, hardly to be distinguish'd from the best of wheat.

Let the turneps first be peel'd, and boil'd in water till soft and tender; then strongly pressing out the juice, mix them together and when dry (beaten or pounded very fine) with their weight of wheat-meal, season it as you do other bread, and knead it up; then letting the dough remain a little to ferment, fashion the paste into loaves, and bake it like common bread.

Some roast turneps in a paper under the embers, and eat them with sugar and butter.

71.   Vine, *Vitis*, the capreols, tendrels and claspers (like those of the hop, &c.) whilst very young, have an agreeable acid, which may be eaten alone, or with other sallet.

---

* *Philos[ophical] Transact[ions]*, Vol. xvii, Num. 205, p. 970.

72.   Viper-grass, *Tragopogon, Scorzonera, Salsifex,* &c. tho' medicinal, and excellent against the palpitation of the heart, faintings, obstruction of the bowels, &c. are besides a very sweet and pleasant sallet; being laid to soak out the bitterness, then peel'd, may be eaten raw, or condited; but best of all stew'd with marrow, spice, wine, &c. as artichoak, skirrets, &c. sliced or whole. They likewise may bake, fry, or boil them; a more excellent root there is hardly growing.

73.   Wood-sorrel, *Trifolium acetosum,* or *Alleluja,* of the nature of other sorrels.

To all which might we add sundry more, formerly had *in deliciis,* since grown obsolete or quite neglected with us: as among the noblest bulbs, that of the tulip; a root of which has been valued not to eat, but for the flower (and yet eaten by mistake) at more than an hundred pounds. The young fresh bulbs are sweet and high of taste.

The asphodil or daffodil; a sallet so rare in Hesiod's days, that Lobel thinks it the parsnep, tho' not at all like it; however it was (with the mallow) taken anciently for any edule-root.

The *ornithogalons* roasted, as they do chestnuts, are eaten by the Italians, the wild yellow especially, with oyl, vinegar, and peper. And so the small tuberous roots of *gramen amygdalosum,* which they also roast, and make an emulsion of, to use in broaths as a great restorative. The *oxylapathum,* not us'd of old; in the time of Galen was eaten frequently. As also *dracontium*, with the mordicant *arum theophrasti*, which Dodonæus teaches how to dress. Nay, divers of the satyrions, which some condited with sugar, others boil'd in milk for a great nourisher, now discarded. But what think we of the *cicuta*, which there are who reckon among sallet herbs? But whatever it is in any other country, 'tis certainly mortiferous in ours. To these add the *viola matronalis, radix lunaria*, &c. nay the green popy, by most accounted among the deadly poysons: how cautious then ought our sallet-gatherers to be, in reading ancient authors; lest they happen to be impos'd on, where they treat of plants, that are familiarly eaten in other countries, and among other nations and people of more robust and strong constitutions? besides the hazard of being mistaken in the names of divers simples, not as yet fully agreed upon among the learned in botany.

There are besides several remaining, which tho' abdicated here with us, find entertainment still in foreign countries: as the large heliotrope and sun-flower (e're it comes to expand, and shew its golden face) which being dress'd as the artichoak, is eaten for a dainty. This I add as a new discovery. I once made macaroons with the ripe blanch'd seeds, but the turpentine did so domineer over all, that it did not answer expectation. The *radix personata* mounting with their young heads. *Lysimachia siliquosa glabra minor*, when fresh and tender, begins to come into the sallet-tribe. The pale whiter popy, is eaten by the Genouese. By the Spaniards, the tops of wormwood with oyl alone, and without so much as bread; profitable indeed to the stomach, but offensive to the head: as is also coriander and rue, which Galen was accustom'd to eat raw, and by it self, with oyl and salt, as exceedingly grateful, as well as wholsome, and of great vertue against infection. Pliny, I remember, reports it to be of such effect for the preservation of sight; that the painters of his time, us'd to devour a great quantity of it. And it is still by the Italians frequently mingled among their sallets. The *lapatha personata* (common burdock) comes now and then to the best tables, about April, and when young, before the burrs and clots appear, being strip'd, and the bitterness soaked out, treated as the chardoon, is eaten in poiverade; some also boil them. More might here be reckon'd up, but these may suffice; since as we find some are left off, and gone out, so others be introduc'd and come in their room, and that in much greater plenty and variety, than was ever known by our ancestors. The cucumber it self, now so universally eaten, being accounted little better than poyson, even within our memory, as already noted.

To conclude, and after all that has been said of plants and salleting, formerly in great esteem, (but since obsolete and quite rejected); what if the exalted juice of the ancient *silphium* should come in, and challenge the precedency? It is a *plant formerly so highly priz'd, and rare for the richness of its taste and other vertues; that as it was dedicated to Apollo, and hung up in his temple at Delphi; so we read of one single root brought to the Emperor Nero for an extraordinary present; and the drug so esteem'd, that the Romans had long before amass'd a quantity of it, and kept it in the treasury, till Julius Cæsar rob'd it, and took this away, as a thing of mighty value: in a word, it was of that account; that as a sacred plant, those of the Cyrenaic Africa, honour'd the very figure of it, by stamping it on the reverse of their ¶coin; and when they would commend a thing for its worth to the skies, BATTOU SILPHION [THE SILPHIUM OF BATTUS], grew into a proverb: Battus having been the founder of the city of Cyrene, near which it only grew. 'Tis indeed contested among the learned botanosophists, whether this plant was not the same with *laserpitium*,

---

* Plin[y], *Nat[uralis] H[istoria]* , Lib. xix, cap. 3. & [Lib.] xx. c[ap]. 22. See Jo[hannes] Tzetzes, *Chil[iades]*, vi. 48. & xvii. 119.
¶ Spanheim, *De Usu & Præst. Numis. Dissert.* 4to. It was sometimes also the reverse of Jupiter Hammon.

46

and the laser it yields, the odoriferous *benzoin? But doubtless had we the true and genuine *silphium* (for it appears to have been often sophisticated, and a spurious sort brought into Italy) it would soon recover its pristine reputation, and that it was not celebrated so for nothing extraordinary; since besides its medicinal vertue; it was a wonderful corroborater of the stomach, a restorer of lost appetite, and masculine vigour, &c. and that they made use of it almost in every thing they eat.

But should we now really tell the world, that this precious juice is, by many, thought to be no other than the ¶foetid assa; our nicer sallet-eaters (who yet bestow as odious an epithet on the vulgar garlick) would cry out upon it as intolerable, and perhaps hardly believe it: but as Aristophanes has brought it in, and sufficiently describ'd it; so the scholiast upon the place, puts it out of controversy: and that they made use both of the leaves, stalk, (and extract especially) as we now do garlick, and other *hautgouts* as nauseous altogether. In the mean time, Garcius, Bontius, and others, assure us, that the Indians at this day universally sauce their viands with it; and the Bramin's (who eat no flesh at all) inrich their sallets, by constantly rubbing the dishes with it. Nor are some of our own skilful cooks ignorant, how to condite and use it, with the applause of those, who, ignorant of the secret, have admir'd the richness of the gust it has imparted, when it has been substituted instead of all our *cipollati*, and other seasonings of that nature.

---

* ————————OUD' AN EI DOIES GE MOI
TON PLOUTON AUTON KAI TO BATTOU SILPHION.
[NOT EVEN IF YOU WERE TO GIVE ME WEALTH HIMSELF AND THE SILPHIUM OF BATTUS],
Aristoph[anes], in *Pluto*, Act iv, Sc. 3.
¶ Of which some would have it a courser sort, *inamœni odoris*, as the same Comedian names it in his *Equites*, p[p].239 and 240, edit. Basil. See likewise this discuss'd, together with its properties, most copiously, in Jo. Budæus a Stapul. *Comment.* in Theophrast[us], lib. vi, cap. 1, and Bauhin, *Hist[oria] Plant[arum] nova et absolutissima]*, lib.xxvii, cap.53.

47

And thus have we done with the various species of all such esculents as may properly enter the composition of our acetaria, and cold sallet. And if I have briefly touch'd upon their natures, degrees and primary qualities, which intend or remit, as to the scale of heat, cold, driness, moisture, &c. (which is to be understood according to the different texture of their component particles) it has not been without what I thought necessary for the instruction of the gatherer, and sallet-dresser; how he ought to choose, sort, and mingle his materials and ingredients together.

What care and circumspection should attend the choice and collection of sallet herbs, has been partly shew'd. I can therefore, by no means, approve of that extravagant fancy of some, who tell us, that a fool is at fit to be the gatherer of a sallet as a wiser man. Because, say they, one can hardly choose amiss, provided the plants be green, young, and tender, where-ever they meet with them: but sad experience shews, how many fatal mistakes have been committed by those who took the deadly *cicutæ*, hemlocks, aconits, &c. for garden persley, and parsneps; the *myrrhis sylvestris*, or cow-weed, for *chærophilum*, (chervil) *thapsia* for fennel; the wild *chondrilla* for succory; dogs-mercury instead of spinach: *papaver corniculatum luteum*, and horn'd poppy for eringo; *oenanthe aquatica* for the palustral *apium*, and a world more, whose dire effects have been many times sudden death, and the cause of mortal accidents to those who have eaten of them unwittingly: but supposing some of those wild and unknown plants should not prove so deleterious and *unwholsome; yet may others of them annoy the head, brain and *genus nervosum*, weaken the eyes, offend the stomach, affect the liver, torment the bowels, and discover their malignity in dangerous and dreadful symptoms. And therefore such plants as are rather

---

* *Vide* Cardanum [Cardan], *De Usu Cibi.*

medicinal than nourishing and refreshing, are studiously to be rejected. So highly necessary it is, that what we sometimes find in old books concerning edules of other countries and climates (frequently call'd by the names of such as are wholsome in ours, and among us) mislead not the unskilful gatherer; to prevent which we read of divers popes and emperors, that had sometimes learned physicians for their master-cooks. I cannot therefore but exceedingly approve of that charitable advice of Mr. Ray *([*Philosophical*]*Transact[ions]* Num. 238.) who thinks it the interest of mankind, that all persons should be caution'd of advent'ring upon unknown herbs and plants to their prejudice: of such, I say, with our excellent ¶poet (a little chang'd)

> Happy from such conceal'd, if still do lie,
> Of Roots and Herbs the unwholsome Luxury.

The illustrious and learned Columna has, by observing what §insects did usually feed on, make [made] conjectures of the nature of the plants. But I should not so readily adventure upon it on that account, as to its wholsomeness: for tho' indeed one may safely eat of a peach or abricot, after a snail has been taster, I question whether it might be so of all other fruits and herbs attack'd by other insects: nor would one conclude, the *hyoscyamus* harmless, because the cimex feeds upon it, as the learned Dr. Lyster has discover'd. Notice should therefore be taken what eggs of insects are found adhering to the leaves of sallet-herbs, and frequently cleave so firmly to them, as not easily to be wash'd off, and so not being taken notice of,

---

* Vol. xx.
¶ Cowley:

OUD' HOSON EN MALACHE TE KAI ASHODELO MEG' ONEIAR
KRUPSANTES HAR ECHOUSI THEOI BION ANTHROPOISI
[NOR HOW GREAT A BENEFIT THERE IS IN MALLOW AND ASPHODEL. FOR THE GODS HAVE HIDDEN THE MEANS OF LIFE FROM MEN], Hesiod, [*Works and Days*].
§ Concerning this of insects, see Mr. Ray's *Hist[oria] Plan[tarum],* li[b]. 1, cap. 24.

passing for accidental and harmless spots only, may yet produce very ill effects.

Grillus, who according to the doctrine of transmigration (as Plutarch tells us) had, in his turn, been a beast; discourses how much better he fed, and liv'd, than when he was turn'd to man again, as knowing then, what plants were best and most proper for him: whilst men, sarcophagists (flesh-eaters) in all this time were yet to seek. And 'tis indeed very evident that cattel, and other PANPHAGA, and herbaceous animals which feed on plants, are directed by their smell, and accordingly make election of their food: but men (besides the smell and taste) have, or should have, reason, experience, and the aids of natural philosophy to be their guides in this matter. We have heard of plants, that (like the basilisk) kill and infect by *looking on them only; and some by the touch. The truth is, there's need of all the senses to determine analogically concerning the vertues and prop–erties, even of the leaves alone of many edule-plants: the most eminent principles of near the whole tribe of sallet vegetables, inclining rather to acid and sowre than to any other quality, especially, salt, sweet, or luscious. There is therefore skill and judgment requir'd, how to suit and mingle our sallet-ingredients, so as may best agree with the constitution of the (vulgarly reputed) humors of those who either stand in need of, or affect these refreshments, and by so adjusting them, that as nothing should be suffer'd to domineer, so should none of them lose their genuine gust, savour, or vertue. To this end,

The cooler, and moderately refreshing, should be chosen to extinguish thirst, attemper the blood, repress vapours, &c.

The hot, dry, aromatic, cordial and friendly to the brain, may be

---

* 'The poyson'd Weeds: I have seen a Man, who was so poyson'd with it, that the Skin peel'd off his Face, and yet he never touch'd it, only looked on it as he pass'd by.' Mr. Stafford, *Philos[ophical] Transact[ions],* Vol. III, Num. xl, p.794.

qualify'd by the cold and moist: the bitter and stomachical, with the sub-acid and gentler herbs: the mordicant and pungent, and such as repress or discuss flatulency (revive the spirits, and aid concoction;) with such as abate, and take off the keenness, mollify and reconcile the more harsh and churlish: the mild and insipid, animated with piquant and brisk: the astringent and binders, with such as are laxative and deobstruct: the over-sluggish, raw, and unactive, with those that are eupeptic, and promote concoction: there are pectorals for the breast and bowels. Those of middle nature, according as they appear to be more or less specific; and as their characters (tho' briefly) are describ'd in our foregoing catalogue: for notwithstanding it seem in general, that raw sallets and herbs have experimentally been found to be the most soveraign diet in that endemial (and indeed with us, epidemical and almost universal) contagion the scorbute, to which we of this nation, and most other ilanders are obnoxious; yet, since the *nasturtia* are singly, and alone as it were, the most effectual, and powerful agents in conquering and expugning that cruel enemy; it were enough to give the sallet-dresser direction how to choose, mingle, and proportion his ingredients; as well as to shew what remedies there are contain'd in our magazine of sallet-plant upon all occasions, rightly marshal'd and skilfully apply'd. So as (with our *sweet Cowley)

> If thro the strong and beauteous Fence
> Of Temperance and Innocence,
> And wholsome Labours, and a quiet Mind,
> Diseases passage find;
> They must not think here to assail
> A Land unarm'd, or without Guard,
> They must fight for it, and dispute it hard,

---

* Cowley, '[The] Garden', *Miscel[lanies]*, Stanz[a] 8.

Before they can prevail;
Scarce any Plant is used here,
Which 'gainst some Aile a Weapon does not bear.

We have said how necessary it is, that in the composure of a sallet, every plant should come in to bear its part, without being over-power'd by some herb of a stronger taste, so as to endanger the native sapor and vertue of the rest; but fall into their places, like the notes in music, in which there should be nothing harsh or grating: and tho' admitting some discords (to distinguish and illustrate the rest) striking in the more sprightly, and sometimes gentler notes, reconcile all dissonancies, and melt them into an agreeable composition. Thus the comical master-cook, introduc'd by Damoxenus, when asked POS ESTIN AUTOIS SUMPHONIA; what harmony there was in meats? The very same (says he) that a diatessaron, diapente, and diapason have one to another in a consort of music: and that there was as great care requir'd, not to mingle *sapores minime consentientes*, jarring and repugnant tastes; looking upon him as a lamentable ignorant, who should be no better vers'd in Democritus. The whole scene is very diverting, as Athenæus presents it; and to the same sense Macrobius, *Saturn[alia]*, lib. 1. cap. 1. In short, the main skill of the artist lies in this:

---

* *Sapores minime consentientes* KAI SUMPLEKOMENAS OUCHI SUMPHONAS HAPHAS [AND HARP-STRINGS INTERWOVEN AND NOT IN HARMONY]: *Hæc despicere ingeniosi est artificis*: Neither did the artist mingle his provisions without extraordinary study and consideration: ALLA MIXAS PANTA KATA SUMPHONIAN [BUT MIXING EVERYTHING TOGETHER IN HARMONY]. *Horum singulis seorsum assumptis, tu expedito: Sic ego tanquam oraculo jubeo.—Itaque literarum ignarum coquum, tu cum videris, & qui Democriti scripta omnia non perlegerit, vel potius, impromptu non habeat, eum deride ut futilem: Ac illum Mercede conducito, qui Epicuri canonem usu plane didicerit,* &c. as it follows in the *Gastronomia* of Archestratus, Athen[aeus], lib. xxiii. Such another bragadoccio cook Horace describes,
   Nec sibi Cænarum quivis temerè arroget artem
   Non prius exactâ tenui ratione saporem.
Sat[ires], Lib. ii, Sat. 4.

> What choice to choose, for delicacy best;
> What Order so contriv'd, as not to mix
> Tastes not well join'd, inelegant, but bring
> Taste after Taste, upheld by kindliest change.

As our *Paradisian Bard introduces Eve, dressing of a sallet for her angelical guest.

Thus, by the discreet choice and mixture of the oxoleon (oyl, vinegar, salt, &c.) the composition is perfect; so as neither the prodigal, niggard, nor insipid, should (according to the Italian rule) prescribe in my opinion; since one may be too profuse, the other ¶over-saving, and the third (like himself) give it no relish at all: it may be too sharp, if it exceed a grateful acid; too insulse and flat, if the profusion be extream. From all which it appears, that a wise-man is the proper composer of an excellent sallet, and how many transcendences belong to an accomplish'd sallet-dresser, so as to emerge an exact critic indeed, he should be skill'd in the degrees, terms, and various species of tastes, according to the scheme set us down in the tables of the learned §Dr. Grew, to which I refer the curious.

'Tis moreover to be consider'd, that edule plants are not in all their tastes and vertues alike: for as providence has made us to consist of different parts and members, both internal and external; so require they different juices to nourish and supply them: wherefore the force and activity of some plants lie in the root; and even the leaves of some bitter-roots are sweet, and *è contra*. Of others, in the stem, leaves, buds, flowers, &c. Some exert their vigour without decoction; others being a little press'd or contus'd; others again raw, and best in

---

* Milton's *Paradise Lost*
¶ ———*Qui*
   Tingat olus siccum muría vafer incalice emptâ,
   Ipse sacrum irrorans piper———
Pers[ius], Sat[ire] vi.
§ Dr. Grew, Lect[ure] vi, c[hapters] 2,3.

consort; some alone and *per se* without any SKEUASIA [PREPARATION], preparation, or mixture at all. Care therefore must be taken by the collector, that what he gathers answer to these qualities; and that as near as he can, they consist (I speak of the cruder salleting) of the *oluscula*, and *ex foliis pubescentibus*, or (as Martial calls them) *prototomi rudes*, and very tenderest parts gems, young buds, and even first rudiments of their several plants; such as we sometimes find in the craws of the wood-culver, stock-dove, partridge, pheasants, and other upland fowl, where we have a natural sallet, pick'd, and almost dress'd to our hands.

I.   Preparatory to the dressing therefore, let your herby ingredients be exquisitely cull'd, and cleans'd of all worm-eaten, slimy, canker'd, dry, spotted, or any ways vitiated leaves. And then that they be rather discreetly sprinkl'd than over-much sob'd with spring-water, especially lettuce, which Dr. *Muffet thinks impairs their vertue; but this, I suppose he means of the cabbage-kind, whose heads are sufficiently protected by the outer leaves which cover it. After washing, let them remain a while in the cullender, to drain the superfluous moisture: and lastly, swing them altogether gently in a clean course napkin; and so they will be in perfect condition to receive the *intinctus* following.

II.   That the oyl, an ingredient so indispensibly and highly necessary, as to have obtain'd the name of *cibarium* (and with us of sallet-oyl) be very clean, not high-colour'd, nor yellow; but with an eye rather of a pallid olive green, without smell, or the least touch of rancid, or indeed of any other sensible taste or scent at all; but smooth, light, and pleasant upon the tongue; such as the genuine omphacine, and native Luca olives afford, fit to allay the tartness of

---

* Muffet, *De Diæta*, c[hapter] 23.

vinegar, and other acids, yet gently to warm and humectate where it passes. Some who have an aversion to oyl, substitute fresh butter in its stead; but 'tis so exceedingly clogging to the stomach, as by no means to be allow'd.

III.   Thirdly, that the vinegar, and other liquid acids, perfectly clear, neither sowre, vapid or spent; be of the best wine vinegar, whether distill'd, or otherwise aromatiz'd, and impregnated with the infusion of clove-gillyflowers, elder, roses, rosemary, nasturtium, &c. inrich'd with the vertues of the plant.

A verjuice not unfit for sallet, is made by a grape of that name, or the green immature clusters of most other grapes, press'd, and put into a small vessel to ferment.

IV.   Fourthly, that the salt (*aliorum condimentorum condimentum*, as Plutarch calls it) detersive, penetrating, quickning (and so great a resister of putrefaction, and universal use, as to have sometimes merited divine epithets) be of the brightest bay grey-salt; moderately dried, and contus'd, as being the least corrosive: but of this, as of sugar also, which some mingle with the salt (as warming without heating) is perfectly refin'd, there would be no great difficulty; provided none, save ladies, were of the mess; whilst the perfection of sallets, and that which gives them the name, consists in the grateful saline acid-point, temper'd as is directed, and which we find to be most esteem'd by judicious palates: some, in the mean time, have been so nice, and luxuriously curious as for the heightning, and (as they affect to speak) giving the utmost poinant and relevèe in lieu of our vulgar salt, to recommend and cry-up the essential-salts and spirits of the most sanative vegetables; or such of the alcalizate and fixt; extracted from the calcination of baulm, rosemary, wormwood, scurvy-grass, &c. Affirming that without the gross plant, we might have healing, cooling, generous, and refreshing cordials, and all the *materia medica* out of the salt-cellar only: but to say no more of this impertinence, as to salts of vegetables; many indeed there be, who reckon them not much unlike in operation, however different in taste, crystals, and figure: it being a question, whether they at all retain the vertues and faculties of their simples, unless they could be made without colcination. Franciscus Redi, gives us his opinion of this, in a process how they are to be prepar'd; and so does our learned *doctor (whom we lately nam'd) whether lixivial, essential, marine, or other factitious salts of plants, with their qualities, and how they differ: but since 'tis thought all fixed salts made the common way, are little better than our common salt, let it suffice, that our sallet-salt be of the best ordinary bay-salt, clean, bright, dry, and without clamminess.

Of sugar (by some call'd Indian-salt) as it is rarely us'd in sallet, it should be of the best refined, white, hard, close, yet light and sweet as the Madera's: nourishing, preserving, cleansing, delighting the taste and preferable to honey for most uses. *Note*, that both this, salt, and vinegar, are to be proportion'd to the constitution, as well as what is said of the plants themselves. The one for cold, the other for hot stomachs.

V. That the mustard (another noble ingredient) be of the best Tewksberry; or else compos'd of the soundest and weightiest Yorkshire seed, exquisitely sifted, winnow'd, and freed from the husks, a little (not over-much) dry'd by the fire, temper'd to the consistence of a pap with vinegar, in which shavings of the horse radish have been steep'd: then cutting an onion, and putting it into a small earthen gally-pot, or some thick glass of that shape; pour the mustard over it, and close it very well with a cork. There be, who

---

* Dr. Grew, *Annat[omy of] Plant[s]*, Lib.i, Sect. iv, cap.i, &c. See also, *[Philosophical] Transact[ions]*, Num. 107, Vol. ix.

preserve the flower and dust of the bruised seed in a well-stopped glass, to temper, and have it fresh when they please. But what is yet by some esteem'd beyond all these, is compos'd of the dried seeds of the Indian nasturtium, reduc'd to powder, finely bolted, and mixt with a little *levain*, and so from time to time made fresh, as indeed all other mustard should be.

Note, that the seeds are pounded in a mortar; or bruis'd with a polish'd cannon-bullet, in a large wooden bowl-dish, or which is most preferr'd, ground in a quern contriv'd for this purpose only.

VI.   Sixthly, that the pepper (white or black) be not bruis'd to too small a dust; which, as we caution'd, is very prejudicial. And here let me mention the root of the *minor pimpinella*, or small burnet saxifrage; which being dried, is by some extoll'd beyond all other peppers, and more wholsom.

Of other strewings and aromatizers, which may likewise be admitted to inrich our sallet, we have already spoken, where we mention orange and limon-peel; to which may also be added, Jamaica-pepper, juniper-berries, &c. as of singular vertue.

Nor here should I omit (the mentioning at least of) saffron, which the German housewives have a way of forming into balls, by mingling it with a little honey; which throughly dried, they reduce to powder, and sprinkle it over their sallets for a noble cordial. Those of Spain and Italy, we know, generally make use of this flower, mingling its golden tincture with almost every thing they eat; but its being so apt to prevail above every thing with which 'tis blended, we little incourage its admittance into our sallet.

VII.   Seventhly, that there be the yolks of fresh and new-laid eggs, boil'd moderately hard, to be mingl'd and mash'd with the mustard, oyl, and vinegar; and part to cut into quarters, and eat with the herbs.

VIII.   Eighthly, (according to the super-curious) that the knife, with which the sallet herbs are cut (especially oranges, limons, &c.) be of silver, and by no means of steel, which all acids are apt to corrode, and retain a metalic relish of.

IX.   Ninthly and lastly, that the *saladiere*, (sallet-dishes) be of porcelane, or of the Holland-Delft-ware; neither too deep nor shallow, according to the quantity of the sallet ingredients; pewter, or even silver, not at all so well agreeing with oyl and vinegar, which leave their several tinctures. And note, that there ought to be one of the dishes, in which to beat and mingle the liquid vehicles; and a second to receive the crude herbs in, upon which they are to be pour'd; and then with a fork and a spoon kept continually stirr'd, 'till all the furniture be equally moisten'd: some, who are husbands of their oyl, pour at first the oyl alone, as more apt to communicate and diffuse its slipperiness, than when it is mingled and beaten with the acids; which they pour on last of all; and 'tis incredible how small a quantity of oyl (in this quality, like the gilding of wyer) is sufficient, to imbue a very plentiful assembly of sallet-herbs.

The sallet-gatherer likewise should be provided with a light, and neatly made withy-Dutch-basket, divided into several partititions.

Thus instructed and knowing in the apparatus; the species, proportions, and manner of dressing, according to the several seasons you have in the following table.

It being one of the inquiries of the noble *Mr Boyle, what herbs were proper and fit to make sallets with, and how best to order them? we have here (by the assistance of Mr. London, His Majesty's Principal Gard'ner) reduc'd them to a competent number, not exceeding thirty five; but which may be vary'd and inlarg'd, by

---

* *Philosoph[ical] Transact[ions],* Vol. III, Num. xl, p.799.

taking-in, or leaving out, any other sallet-plant, mention'd in the fore-going list, under these three or four heads.

But all these sorts are not be had at the very same time, and therefore we have divided them into the quarterly seasons, each containing and lasting three months.

Note, that by parts is to be understood a pugil; which is no more than one does usually take up between the thumb and the two next fingers. By fascicule a reasonable full grip, or handful.

[The table is on pp. xvii and xviii of this edition.]

Farther Directions concerning the proper Seasons, *for the* Gathering, Composing, *and* Dressing *of a* Sallet.

AND first, as to the season, both plants and roots are then properly to be gather'd, and in prime, when most they abound with juice and in vigour: some in the spring, or a little anticipating it before they blossom, or are in full flower: some in the autumnal months; which later season many preferr, the sap of the herb, tho' not in such exuberance, yet as being then better concocted, and so render'd fit for salleting, 'till the spring begins a fresh to put forth new, and tender shoots and leaves.

This, indeed, as to the root, newly taken out of the ground is true; and therefore should such have their germination stopt the sooner: the approaching and prevailing cold, both maturing and impregnating them; as does heat the contrary, which now would but exhaust them: but for those other esculents and herbs imploy'd in our composition of sallets, the early spring, and ensuing months (till they begin to mount, and prepare to seed) is certainly the most natural, and kindly season to collect and accommodate them for the table. Let none then consult Culpeper, or the figure flingers, to inform them when the governing planet is in its exaltation; but look upon the plants themselves, and judge of their vertues by their own complexions.

Moreover, in gathering, respect is to be had to their proportions, as provided for in the table under that head, be the quality whatsoever: for tho' there is indeed nothing more wholsome than lettuce and mustard for the head and eyes; yet either of them eaten in excess, were highly prejudicial to them both: too much of the first extreamly debilitating and weakning the ventricle, and hastning the further decay of sickly teeth; and of the second the optic nerves, and sight it self; the like may be said of all the rest. I conceive therefore, a prudent person, well acquainted with the nature and properties of sallet-herbs, &c. to be both the fittest gatherer and composer too; which yet will require no great cunning, after once he is acquainted with our table and catalogue.

We purposely, and *in transitu* only, take notice here of the pickl'd, muriated, or otherwise prepared herbs; excepting some such plants, and proportions of them, as are of hard digestion, and not fit to be eaten altogether crude, (of which in the Appendix) and among which I reckon ash-keys, broom-buds and pods, haricos, gurkems, olives, capers, the buds and seeds of nasturtia, young wall-nuts, pine-apples, eringo, cherries, cornelians, berberries, &c. together with several stalks, roots, and fruits; ordinary pot-herbs, anis, *cistus hortorum, horminum, pulegium, satureia,* thyme; the intire family of pulse and *legumena*; or other sauces, pies, tarts, omlets, tansie, farces, &c. condites and preserves with sugar by the hand of ladies; tho' they are all of them the genuine production of the garden, and mention'd in our *Kalendar,* together with their culture; whilst we confine our selves to such plants and esculenta as we find at hand; delight our selves to gather, and are easily prepar'd for an extemporary collation, or to usher in, and accompany other (more solid, tho' haply not more agreeable) dishes, as the custom is.

But there now starts up a question, whether it were better, or more proper, to begin with sallets, or end and conclude with them? Some think the harder meats should first be eaten for better concoction; others, those of easiest digestion, to make way, and prevent obstruction; and this makes for our sallets, *horarii,* and *fugaces fructus* (as they call 'em) to be eaten first of all, as agreeable to the general opinion of the great Hippocrates, and Galen, and of Celsus before him. And therefore the French do well, to begin with their herbaceous pottage, and for the cruder, a reason is given:

Prima tibi dabitur Ventri Lactuca movendo
Utilis, & Poris fila resecta suis.

And tho' this custom came in about Domitian's time[1], HO [HOI] MEN ARCHAIOI [THE ANCIENTS], they anciently did quite the contrary,

§*Gratáque nobilium Lactuca ciborum .*

But of later times, they were constant at the *ante-cœnia*, eating plentifully of sallet, especially of lettuce, and more refrigerating herbs. Nor without cause: for drinking liberally, they were found to expell, and allay the fumes and vapors of the genial compotation, the spirituous liquor gently conciliating sleep: besides, that being of a crude nature, more dispos'd, and apt to fluctuate, corrupt, and disturb and surcharg'd stomach; they thought convenient to begin with sallets, and innovate the ancient usage.

#——*Nam Lactuca innatat acri*
Post Vinum Stomacho——

For if on drinking Wine you Lettuce eat,
It floats upon the Stomach—

The Spaniards, notwithstanding, eat but sparingly of herbs at dinner, especially lettuce, beginning with fruit, even before the olio and hot-meats come to the table; drinking their wine pure, and eating the best bread in the world; so as it seems the question still remains undecided with them,

---

* Mart[ial], *Epig[rams]*, lib. xi, [Epigram] 39.
¶ Athen[aeus], l[ib.] 2. Of which change of diet see Plut[arch] iv. *Sympos[iaca]*, 9. Plinii, *Epist[olae]*, i, *ad Eretrium*.
§ Virg[il], *Moreto [Moretum]*.
# Hor[ace], *Sat[ires]*, l[ib.] 2, Sat[ire] 4.

*Claudere quæ cœnas lactuca solebat avorum
Dic mihi cur nostras inchoat illa dapes?*

· The Sallet, which of old came in at last,
Why now with it begin we our Repast?

And now since we mention'd fruit, there rises another scruple: whether apples, pears, abricots, cherries, plums, and other tree, and ort-yard-fruit, are to be reckon'd among salleting; and when likewise most seasonably to be eaten? But as none of these do properly belong to our catalogue of herbs and plants, to which this discourse is confin'd (besides what we may occasionally speak of hereafter) there is a very useful ¶treatise on that subject already publish'd. We hasten then in the next place to the dressing, and composing of our sallet: for by this time, our scholar may long to see the rules reduc'd to practice, and refresh himself with what he finds growing among his own *lactuceta* and other beds of the kitchin-garden.

---

* Mart[ial], *Ep[igrams]*, l[ib]. v, Ep[igram] 17.
¶ *Concerning the Use of Fruit (besides many others) whether best to be eaten before, or after Meals?* Published by a Physician of Rochel, and render'd out of French into English. Printed by T. Basset in Fleetstreet.

DRESSING.

I AM not ambitious of being thought an excellent cook, or of those who set up, and value themselves, for their skill in sauces: such as was Mithacus a culinary philosopher, and other *eruditæ gulæ*; who read lectures of *hautgouts*, like the Archestratus in Athenæus: tho' after what we find the heroes did of old, and see them chining out the slaughter'd ox, dressing the meat, and do the offices of both cook and butcher, (for so [*]Homer represents Achilles himself, and the rest of those illustrious Greeks) I say, after this, let none reproach our sallet-dresser, or disdain so clean, innocent, sweet and natural a quality; compar'd with the shambles filth and nidor, blood and cruelty; whilst all the world were eaters, and composers of sallets in its best and brightest age.

The ingredients therefore gather'd and proportion'd, as above; let the endive have all its out-side leaves stripp'd off, slicing in the white: in like manner the sellery is also to have the hollow green stem or stalk trimm'd and divided; slicing-in the blanched part, and cutting the root into four equal parts.

Lettuce, cresses, radish, &c. (as was directed) must be exquisitely pick'd, cleans'd, wash'd, and put into the strainer; swing'd, and shaken gently, and, if you please, separately, or all together; because some like not so well the blanch'd and bitter herbs, if eaten with the rest: others mingle endive, succory, and rampions, without distinction, and generally eat sellery by it self, as also sweet fennel.

From April till September (and during all the hot months) may Guinny-pepper, and horse-radish be left out; and therefore we only mention them in the dressing, which should be in this manner.

---

[*] Achilles, Patroclus, Automedon, *Iliad.* ix, & *alibi.*

Your herbs being handsomly parcell'd, and spread on a clean napkin before you, are to be mingl'd together in one of the earthen glaz'd dishes: then, for the oxoleon; take of clear, and perfectly good oyl-olive, three parts; of sharpest vinegar (*sweetest of all condiments) limon, or juice of orange, one part; and therein let steep some slices of horse-radish, with a little salt: some in a separate vinegar, gently bruise a pod of Guinny-pepper, straining both the vinegars apart, to make use of either, or one alone, or of both, as they best like; then add as much Tewkesbury, or other dry mustard grated, as will lie upon an half-crown piece: beat, and mingle all these very well together; but pour not on the oyl and vinegar, 'till immediately before the sallet is ready to be eaten: and then with the yolk of two new-laid eggs (boyl'd and prepar'd, as before is taught) squash, and bruise them all into mash with a spoon; and lastly, pour it all upon the herbs, stirring, and mingling them 'till they are well and throughly imbib'd; not forgetting the sprinklings of aromaticks, and such flowers, as we have already mentioned, if you think fit, and garnishing the dish with the thin slices of horse-radish, red beet, berberries, &c.

Note, that the liquids may be made more, or less acid, as is most agreeable to your taste.

These rules, and prescriptions duly observ'd; you have a sallet (for a table of six or eight persons) dress'd and accommodated *secundum artem*: for, as the ¶proverb has it,

OU PANTOS ANDROS ESTIN ARTUSAI KALOS.

[IT IS NOT FOR EVERY MAN TO SEASON WELL]

Non est cujusvis rectè condire.

---

* For so some pronounce it. *V.* Athenæum [Athenæus] *Deip[nosophistai]*, Lib.II, Cap. 26, EDOS [DELIGHT] *quasi* HEDUSMA [SEASONING] perhaps for that it incites appetite, and causes hunger, which is the best sauce.
¶ Cratinus in *Glauco*.

AND now after all we have advanc'd in favour of the herbaceous diet, there still emerges a third inquiry; namely whether the use of crude herbs and plants are so wholesom as is pretended?

What opinion the Prince of Physicians had of them, we shall see hereafter; as also what the sacred records of elder times seem to infer, before there were any flesh-shambles in the world; together with the report of such as are often conversant among many nations and people, who to this day, living on herbs and roots, arrive to incredible age, in constant health and vigour: which, whether attributable to the air and climate, custom, constitution, &c. should be inquir'd into; especially, when we compare the antediluvians mention'd Gen[esis] 1.29—the whole fifth and ninth chapters, ver. 3. confining them to fruit and wholesom sallets: I deny not that both the air and earth might then be less humid and clammy, and consequently plants and herbs better fermented, concocted and less rheumatick, than since, and presently after; to say nothing of the infinite numbers of putrid carcasses of dead animals, perishing in the flood, (of which I find few, if any, have taken notice) which needs must have corrupted the air: those who live in marshes, and uliginous places (like the Hundreds of Essex) being more obnoxious to fevers, agues, pleurisies, and generally unhealthful: the earth also then a very bog, compar'd with what it likely was before that destructive cataclism, when men breath'd the pure paradisian air, sucking in a more æthereal, nourishing, and baulmy pabulum, so foully vitiated now, thro' the intemperance, luxury, and softer education and effeminacy of the ages since.

Custom, and constitution come next to be examin'd, together with the qualities, and vertue of the food; and I confess, the two first, especially that of constitution, seems to me the more likely cause of health, and consequently of long-life; which induc'd me to consider of what quality the usual sallet furniture did more eminently consist, that so it might become more safely applicable to the temper, humour, and disposition of our bodies; according to which, the various mixtures might be regulated and proportion'd: there's no doubt, but those whose constitutions are cold and moist, are naturally affected with things which are hot and dry; as on the contrary, hot, and dry complexions, with such as cool and refrigerate; which perhaps made the Junior Gordian (and others like him) prefer the *frigidæ mensæ* (as of old they call'd sallets) which, according to Cornelius Celsus, is the fittest diet for obese and corpulent persons, as not so nutritive, and apt to pamper: and consequently, that for the cold, lean, and emaciated; such herby ingredients should be made choice of, as warm, and cherish the natural heat, de-pure the blood, breed a laudable juice, and revive the spirits and therefore my Lord *Bacon shews what are best raw, what boil'd, and what parts of plants fittest to nourish. Galen indeed seems to exclude them all, unless well accompanied with their due correctives, of which we have taken care: notwithstanding yet, that even the most crude and herby, actually cold and weak, may potentially be hot, and strengthning, as we find in the most vigorous animals, whose food is only grass. 'Tis true indeed, nature has providentially mingl'd, and dress'd a sallet for them in every field, besides what they distinguish by smell; nor question I, but man at first knew what plants and fruits were good, before the fall, by his natural sagacity, and not experience; which since by art, and trial, and long observation of their properties and effects, they hardly recover: but in all events, supposing with ¶Cardan, that plants nourish little, they hurt as little. Nay, experience tells us, that they not only hurt not at all, but exceeedingly benefit those who use them;

---

* [Bacon], *Nat[ural] Hist[ory]*, IV. Cent. VII, 130. Se[e] Arist[otle], *Prob[lems]*, Sect. xx, Quæst. 36. Why some fruits and plants are best raw, others boil'd, roasted, &c, as becoming sweeter; but the crude more sapid and grateful.
¶ Card[an], *Contradicent. Med.,* l[ib]. iv, cant. 18. Diphilus not at all, Athenæus.

indu'd as they are with such admirable properties as they every day discover: for some plants not only nourish laudably, but induce a manifest and wholesom change; as onions, garlick, rochet, &c. which are both nutritive and warm; lettuce, purselan, the intybs, &c. and indeed most of the *olera*, refresh and cool: and as their respective juice being converted into the substances of our bodies, they become aliment; so in regard of their change and alteration, we may allow them medicinal; especially the greater numbers, among which we all this while have skill but of very few (not only in the vegetable kingdom, but in the whole *materia medica*) which may be justly call'd infallible specifics, and upon whose performance we may as safely depend, as we may on such as familiarly we use for a crude herb-sallet; discreetly chosen, mingl'd, and dress'd accordingly: not but that many of them may be improv'd, and render'd better in broths, and decoctions, than in oyl, vinegar, and other liquids and ingredients: but as this holds not in all, nay, perhaps in few comparatively, (provided, as I said, the choice, mixture, constitution, and season rightly be understood) we stand up in defence and vindication of our sallet, against all attacks and opposers whoever.

We have mentioned season, and with the great Hippocrates, pronounce them more proper for the summer, than the winter; and when those parts of plants us'd in sallet are yet tender, delicate, and impregnated with the vertue of the spring, to cool, refresh, and allay the heat and drought of the hot and bilious, young and over-sanguine, cold, pituit, and melancholy; in a word, for persons of all ages, humours, and constitutions whatsoever.

To this of the annual seasons, we add that of culture also, as of very great importance: and this is often discover'd in the taste, and consequently, in the goodness of such plants and salletting, as are rais'd and brought us fresh out of the country, compar'd with those which the avarice of the gardiner, or luxury rather of the age, tempts them to force and resuscitate of the most desirable and delicious plants.

It is certain, says a *learned person, that about populous cities, where grounds are over-forc'd for fruit and early salletting, nothing is more unwholsom: men in the country look so much more healthy and fresh; and commonly are longer liv'd than those who dwell in the middle and skirts of vast and crowded cities, inviron'd with rotten dung, loathsome and common lay-stalls; whose noisome steams, wafted by the wind, poison and infect the ambient air and vital spirits, with those pernicious exhalations, and materials of which they make the hot beds for the raising those *præcoces* indeed, and forward plants and roots for the wanton palate; but which being corrupt in the original, cannot but produce malignant and ill effects to those who feed upon them. And the same was well observ'd by the editor of our famous Roger Bacon's treatise concerning the *Cure of Old Age*, and *Preservation of Youth*: there being nothing so proper for sallet herbs and other edule plants, as the genial and natural mould impregnate, and enrich'd with well digested compost (when requisite) without any mixture of garbage, odious carrion, and other filthy ordure, not half consum'd and ventilated and indeed reduc'd to the next disposition of earth it self, as it should be; and that in sweet, ¶rising, aery and moderately perflatile grounds; where not only plants but men do last, and live much longer. Nor doubt I, but that every body would prefer corn, and other grain rais'd from marle, chalk, lime, and other sweet soil and amendments, before that which is produc'd from the dunghil only[.] Beside, experience shews, that the rankness of dung is frequently the cause of blasts and smuttiness; as if the lord of the universe, by an act of visible providence would check us, to

---

* Sir Tho. Brown's *Miscel[lany Tracts]*.
¶ *Caule suburbano qui siccis crevit in agris Dulcior.* —Hor[ace], *Sat[ires]*, l[ib].
  2, §.4.

take heed of all unnatural sordidness and mixtures. We sensibly find this difference in cattle and their pasture; but most powerfully in fowl, from such as are nourish'd with corn, sweet and dry food: and as of vegetable meats, so of drinks, 'tis observ'd, that the same vine, according to the soil, produces a wine twice as heady as in the same, and a less forc'd ground; and the like I believe of all other fruit, not to determine anything of the peach said to be poison in Persia; because 'tis a vulgar error.

Now, because among other things, nothing more betrays its unclean and spurious birth than what is so impatiently longed after as early asparagus, &c. *Dr. Lister, (according to his communicative and obliging nature) has taught us how to raise such as our gardiners cover with nasty litter, during the winter; by rather laying of clean and sweet wheat-straw upon the beds, super-seminating and over-strowing them thick with the powder of bruised oyster-shells, &c. to produce that most tender and delicious sallet. In the mean while, if nothing will satisfie save what is rais'd *ex tempore*, and by miracles of art so long before the time; let them study (like the *adepti*) as did a very ingenious gentleman whom I knew; that having some friends of his accidentally come to dine with him, and wanting an early sallet, before they sate down to table, sowed lettuce and some other seeds in a certain composition of mould he had prepared; which within the space of two hours, being risen near two inches high, presented them with a delicate and tender sallet; and this, without making use of any nauseous and fulsome mixture; but of ingredients not altogether so cheap perhaps. Honoratus Faber (no mean philosopher) shews us another method by sowing the seeds steep'd in vinegar, casting on it a good quantity of bean-shell ashes, irrigating them with spirit of wine, and keeping the beds well cover'd under dry matts. Such another process for the raising early peas and beans, &c. we have the

---

* *Philos[ophical] Transact[ions]* , Num. xxv.

like *accounts of: but were they practicable and certain, I confess I should not be fonder of them, than of such as the honest industrious country-man's field, and good-wife's garden seasonably produce; where they are legitimately born in just time, and without forcing nature.

But to return again to health and long life, and the wholesomness of the herby-diet, ¶John Beverovicius, a learn'd physician (out of Peter Moxa, a Spaniard) treating of the extream age, which those of America usually arrive to, asserts in behalf of crude and natural herbs: Diphilus of old, as §Athenæus tells us, was on the other side, against the tribe of *olera* in general; and Cardan of late (as already noted) no great friend to them; affirming flesh-eaters to be much wiser and more sagacious. But this his #learned antagonist utterly denies; whole nations, flesh-devourers (such as farthest northern) becoming heavy, dull, unactive, and much more stupid than the southern; and such as feed much on plants, are more acute, subtil, and of deeper penetration: witness the Chaldæans, Assyrians, Ægyptians, &c. And further argues from the short lives of most carnivorous animals, compared with grass feeders, and the ruminating kind; as the hart, camel, and the longævous elephant, and other feeders on roots and vegetables.

I know what is pretended of our bodies being composed of dissimilar parts, and so requiring variety of food: nor do I reject the opinion, keeping to the same species; of which there is infinitely more variety in the herby family, than in all nature besides: but the danger is in the generical difference of flesh, fish, fruit, &c. with other made dishes and exotic sauces; which a wanton and expensive luxury has

---

* *[Ibid.]*, Num. xviii.
¶ *Thesaur[us] Sanit[atis]*, c[ap]. 2.
§ As Delcampius interprets the place.
# [Julius Caesar] Scaliger, *ad Card[anus] Exercit[ationes]*, 213.

71

introduc'd; debauching the stomach, and sharpening it to devour
things of such difficult concoction, with those of more easie digestion, and of contrary substances, more than it can well dispose of:
otherwise food of the same kind would do us little hurt: so true is that
of *Celsus, *Eduntur facilius; ad concoctionem autem materiæ, genus,
& modus pertineat.* They are (says he) easily eaten and taken in: but
regard should be had to their digestion, nature, quantity and quality
of the matter. As to that of dissimilar parts, requiring this contended-
for variety: if we may judge by other animals (as I know not why we
may not) there is (after all the late contests about comparative anat-
omy) so little difference in the structure, as to the use of those parts
and vessels destin'd to serve the offices of concoction, nutrition, and
other separations for supply of life, &c. That it does not appear why
there should need any difference at all of food; of which the most
simple has ever been esteem'd the best, and most wholsome;
according to that of the ¶Naturalist, *hominis cibus utilissimus simplex.*
And that so it is in other animals, we find by their being so seldom
afflicted with mens distempers, deriv'd from the causes above-
mentioned: and if the many diseases of horses seem to §contradict
it, I am apt to think it much imputable to the rack and manger, the
dry and wither'd stable commons, which they must eat or starve,
however qualified; being restrained from their natural and
spontaneous choice, which nature and instinct directs them to: to
these add the closeness of the air, standing in an almost continu'd
posture; besides the fulsome drenches, unseasonable watrings, and
other practices of ignorant horse-quacks and surly grooms: the
tyranny and cruel usage of their masters in tiring journeys, hard,

---

* Cel[sus, *Artes*], Lib. [-], Cap. 4.
¶ Plin[y], *Nat. Hist.*, l[ib.] 3, c[ap.] 12.
§ *Hanc brevitatem Vitæ* (speaking of horses) *fortasse homini debet,* Verul[am],
  Hist[oria] Vit[ae] & Mort[is], see this throughly controverted, Macrob[ius],
  Saturn[alia], l[ib]. vii, c[ap]. v.

labouring and unmerciful treatment, heats, colds, &c. which wear out
and destroy so many of those useful and generous creatures before
the time: such as have been better us'd, and some, whom their more
gentle and good-natur'd patrons have in recompence of their long and
faithful service, dismiss'd, and sent to pasture for the rest of their
lives (as the Grand-Seignior does his Meccha-camel) have been
known to live forty, fifty, nay (says *Aristotle[)], no fewer than sixty
five years. When once Old Par came to change his simple, homely
diet, to that of the court and Arundel-House, he quickly sunk and
dropt away: for, as we have shew'd, the stomack easily concocts
plain, and familiar food; but finds it an hard and difficult task, to
vanquish and overcome meats of ¶different substances: whence we
so often see temperate and abstemious persons, of a collegiate diet,
very healthy; husbandmen and laborious people, more robust, and
longer liv'd than others of an uncertain extravagant diet.

§ ——*Nam variæ res*
Ut noceant Homini, credas, memor illius escæ,
Que simplex olim tibi sederit——

For different Meats do hurt; Remember how
When to one Dish confin'd, thou healthier wast than now:

was Osellus's memorandum in the Poet.

   Not that variety (which God has certainly ordain'd to delight and
assist our appetite) is unnecessary, nor any thing more grateful,
refreshing and proper for those especially who lead sedentary and
studious lives; men of deep thought, and such as are otherwise
disturb'd with secular cares and businesses, which hinders the

---

* Arist[otle], *Hist[oria] Animal[ium]*, l[ib]. v, c[ap]. 14.
¶ ANOMOIA SASIAZEI
§ Hor[ace], *Sat[ires]*, l[ib]. II, Sat[ire] 2; Macr[obius], *Sat[urnalia]*, l[ib]. VII.

function of the stomach and other organs: whilst those who have their minds free, use much exercise, and are more active, create themselves a natural appetite, which heeds little or no variety to quicken and content it.

And here might we attest the patriarchal world, nay, and many persons since; who living very temperately came not much short of the post-diluvians themselves, counting from Abraham to this day; and some exceeding them, who liv'd in pure air, a constant, tho' course and simple diet; wholsome and uncompounded drink; that never tasted brandy or exotic spirits; but us'd moderate exercise, and observ'd good hours: for such a one a curious missionary tells us of in Persia; who had attain'd the age of four hundred years, (a full century beyond the famous Johannes de Temporibus) and was living *anno* 1636 and so may be still for ought we know. But, to our sallet.

Certain it is, Almighty God ordaining *herbs and fruit for the food of men, speaks not a word concerning flesh for two thousand years. And when after, by the Mosaic constitution, there were distinctions and prohibitions about the legal uncleanness of animals; plants, of what kind soever, were left free and indifferent for every one to choose what best he lik'd. And what if it was held undecent and unbecoming the excellency of man's nature, before sin entred, and grew enormously wicked, that any creature should be put to death and pain for him who had such infinite store of the most delicious and nourishing fruit to delight, and the Tree of Life to sustain him? Doubtless there was no need of it. Infants sought the mother's nipple as soon as born; and when grown, and able to feed themselves, run naturally to fruit, and still will choose to eat it rather than flesh and certainly might so persist to do, did not custom prevail, even against the very dictates of nature: nor, question I, but that what the heathen

---

* *Gen[esis]*, ix.

*poets recount of the happiness of the golden age, sprung from some tradition they had received of the paradisian fare, their innocent and healthful lives in that delightful garden. Let it suffice, that Adam, and his yet innocent spouse, fed on vegetables and other hortulan productions before the fatal lapse; which, by the way, many learned men will hardly allow to have fallen out so soon as those imagine who scarcely grant them a single day; nay, nor half a one, for their continuance in the state of original perfection; whilst the sending him into the garden; instructions how he should keep and cultivate it; edict, and prohibition concerning the sacramental trees; the imposit-ion of ¶names, so apposite to the nature of such an infinity of living creatures (requiring deep inspection) the formation of Eve, a meet companion to relieve his solitude; the solemnity of their marriage; the dialogues and success of the crafty Tempter, who we cannot reas-onably think made but one assault: and that they should so quickly forget the injunction of their maker and benefactor; break their faith and fast, and all other their obligations in so few moments. I say, all these particulars consider'd; can it be supposed they were so soon transacted as those do fancy, who take their measure from the summary Moses gives us, who did not write to gratifie mens curios-ity, but to transmit what was necessary and sufficient for us to know.

This then premis'd (as I see no reason why it should not) and that during all this space they liv'd on fruits and sallets; 'tis little probable, that after their transgression, and that they had forfeited their dominion over the creature (and were sentenc'd and exil'd to a life of sweat and labour on a cursed and ungrateful soil) the offended God should regale them with pampering flesh, or so much as suffer them to slay the more innocent animal: or, that if at any time they had permission, it was for any thing save skins to cloath them, or in

---

* [Ovid], *Metam[orphoses]*, I, Fab. iii and xv.
¶ *Gen[esis]*, xi, 19.

way of adoration, or holocaust for expiation, of which nothing of the flesh was to be eaten. Nor did the brutes themselves subsist by prey (tho' pleas'd perhaps with hunting, without destroying their fellow creatures) as may be presum'd from their long seclusion of the most carnivorous among them in the ark.

Thus then for two thousand years, the universal food was herbs and plants; which abundantly recompens'd the want of flesh and other luxurious meats, which shortened their lives so many hundred years; the *MAKROBIOTETA [LONGEVITY] of the patriarchs, which was an emblem of eternity as it were (after the new concession) beginning to dwindle to a little span, a nothing in comparison.

On the other side, examine we the present usages of several other heathen nations; particularly (besides the Ægyptian priests of old) the Indian bramins, relicts of the ancient Gymnosophists to this day, observing the institutions of their founder. Flesh, we know was banish'd the Platonic tables, as well as from those of Pythagoras; (see ¶Porphyry and their disciples) tho' on different accounts. Among others of the philosophers, from Xenocrates, Polemon, &c. we hear of many. The like we find in §Clement Alexand. #Eusebius names more. Zeno, Archinomus, Phraartes, Chiron, and others, whom Laertius reckons up. In short, so very many, especially of the Christian profession, that some, even of the ancient †fathers themselves, have almost thought that the permission of eating flesh to Noah and his sons, was granted them no otherwise than repudiation of wives was to the Jews, namely for the hardness of their hearts, and to satisfie a murmuring generation that a little after loathed manna

---

* Gen[esis], ix.
¶ Porphyr[y], De abstin[entia], Proclum [Proclus], Jambleum [Iamblichus], &c.
§ [Clement of Alexandria], Strom[ateis], vii.
# Præp[aratio] Ev[angelica], passim.
† Tertul[lian], de Jejun[io], cap. iv; Hieron[ymus] [i.e. St. Jerome], Advers[us] Jovin[ianum].

it self, and bread from heaven. So difficult a thing it is to subdue an unruly appetite; which notwithstanding *Seneca thinks not so hard a task; where speaking of the philosopher Sextius, and Socion's (abhorring cruelty and intemperance) he celebrates the advantages of the herby and sallet diet, as physical, and natural advancers of health and other blessings; whilst abstinence from flesh deprives men of nothing but what lions, vultures, beasts and birds of prey, blood and gorge themselves withal. The whole epistle deserves the reading, for the excellent advice he gives on this and other subjects; and how from many troublesome and slavish impertinencies, grown into habit and custom (old as he was) he had emancipated and freed himself: be this apply'd to our present excessive drinkers of foreign and exotic liquors. And now

I am sufficiently sensible how far, and to how little purpose I am gone on this topic: the ply is long since taken, and our raw sallet deckt in its best trim, is never like to invite men who once have tasted flesh to quit and abdicate a custom which has now so long obtain'd. Nor truly do I think conscience at all concern'd in the matter, upon any account of distinction of pure and impure; tho' seriously consider'd (as Sextius held) *rationi magis congrua*, as it regards the cruel butcheries of so many harmless creatures; some of which we put to merciless and needless torment, to accommodate them for exquisite and uncommon Epicurism. There lies else no positive prohibition; discrimination of meats being ¶condemn'd as the doctrine of devils: nor do meats commend us to God. One eats *quid vult* (of every thing) another *olera*, and of sallets only: but this is not my business, further than to shew how possible it is by so many instances and examples, to live on wholsome vegetables, both long and happily: for so

---

* Sen[eca], *Epist[ulae morales]*, 108.
¶ I.Cor[inthians], viii, 8; I.Tim[othy], iv, 1, 3, 14; Rom[ans], ii, 3.

*The Golden Age, with this Provision blest,
Such a Grand Sallet made, and was a Feast.
The Demi-Gods with Bodies large and sound,
Commended then the Product of the Ground.
Fraud then, nor Force were known, nor filthy Lust,
Which Over-heating and Intemp'rance nurst:
Be their vile Names in Execration held,
Who with foul Glutt'ny first the World defil'd:
Parent of Vice, and all Diseases since,
With ghastly Death sprung up alone from thence.
Ah, from such reeking, bloody Tables fly,
Which Death for our Destruction does supply.
In Health, if Sallet Herbs you can't endure;
Sick, you'll desire them; or for Food, or Cure.

As to the other part of the controversie, which concerns us,
HAIMATOPHAGOI [BLOOD-EATERS], and occidental blood-eater;, some
grave and learn'd men of late seem to scruple the present usage,
whilst they see the prohibition appearing, and to carry such a face

---

* *Has Epulas habuit teneri gens aurea mundi,*
  Et cœnæ ingentis tunc caput ipsa sui.
Semideumque meo creverunt corpora succo,
  Materiam tanti sanguinis ille dedit.
Tunc neque fraus nota est, neque vis, neque fœda libido;
  Hæc nimis proles sæva caloris erat.
Sit sacrum illorum, sit detestabile nomen,
  Qui primi servæ regna dedere gulæ.
Hinc vitiis patefacta via est, morbisq; secutis
  Se lethi facies exeruere novæ.
Ah, fuge crudeles Animantum sanguine mensas,
  Quasque tibi obsonat mors inimica dapes.
Poscas tandem æger, si sanus negligis, herbas.
  Esse cibus nequeunt? at medicamen erunt.
Colci *Plaut.* [*recte* Cowley, *Plantarum*], lib. I, *Lactuca.*

of antiquity, *scripture, ¶councils,§canons, †fathers; imperial constitutions, and universal practice, unless it be among us of these tracts of Europe, whither, with other barbarities, that of eating the blood and animal life of creatures first was brought; and by our mixtures with the Goths, Vandals and other spawn of pagan Scythians; grown a custom, and since which I am persuaded more blood has been shed between Christians than there ever was before the water of the flood covered this corner of the world: not that I impute it only to our eating blood; but sometimes wonder how it hapned that so strict, so solemn and famous a sanction not upon a ceremonial account; but (as some affirm) a moral and perpetual from Noah, to whom the concession of eating flesh was granted, and that of blood forbidden (nor to this day once revok'd) and whilst there also seems to lie fairer proofs than for most other controversies agitated among Christians, should be so generally forgotten, and give place to so many other impertinent disputes and cavels about other superstitious fopperies, which frequently end in blood and cutting of throats.

As to the reason of this prohibition, its favouring of cruelty excepted, (and that by Galen, and other experienc'd physicians, the eating blood is condemn'd as unwholsome, causing indigestion and obstructions) if a positive command of Almighty God were not enough, it seems sufficiently intimated; because blood was the vehicle of the life and animal soul of the creature: for what other mysterious cause, as haply its being always dedicated to expiatory

---

* *Gen[esis]*, ix.
¶ [Synod of] Ancyra, xiv.
§ Can. Apost.[Apostolic Canons], 50.
† Clem[ent of Alexandria], *Pædag[ogus]*, Lib. II, c[ap]. i. *Vide* Prudent[ius'] hymn, KATHEMERINON [THE DAILY ROUND]: *Nos Oloris Coma, nos filiqua facta legumine multitudo paraveris innocuis Epulis.*

sacrifices, &c. it is not for us to enquire. 'Tis said, that *Justin Martyr being asked, why the Christians of his time were permitted the eating flesh and not the blood? readily answer'd, that God might distinguish them from beasts, which eat them both together. 'Tis likewise urg'd, that by the apostolical synod (when the rest of the Jewish ceremonies and types were abolish'd) this prohibition was mention'd as a thing ¶necessary, and rank'd with idolatry, which was not to be local or temporary; but universally injoyn'd to converted strangers and proselytes, as well as Jews: nor could the scandal of neglecting to observe it, concern them alone, after so many ages as it was and still is in continual use; and those who transgress'd, so severely punish'd, as by an imperial law to be scourg'd to blood and bone: indeed, so terrible was the interdiction, that idolatry excepted (which was also moral and perpetual) nothing in scripture seems to be more express. In the mean time, to relieve all other scruples, it does not, they say, extend to that AKRIBEIA of those few diluted drops of extravasated blood, which might happen to tinge the juice and gravy of the flesh (which were indeed to strain at a gnat) but to those who devour the venal and arterial blood separately, and in quantity, as a choice ingredient of their luxurious preparations and Apician tables.

But this, and all the rest will, I fear, seem but *oleribus verba facere*, and (as the proverb goes) be labour-in-vain to think of preaching down hogs-puddings, and usurp the chair of Rabby-Busy: and therefore what is advanc'd in countenance of the antediluvian diet, we leave to be ventilated by the learned, and such as Curcellæus, who has borrow'd of all the ancient fathers, from Tertullian, Hierom [Jerome], S. Chrysostom, &c. to the later doctors and divines, Lyra, Tostatus, Dionysius Carthusianus, Pererius, amongst the pontificians;

---

* [Justin Martyr,] *Quæst. & Resp.ad Orthod. [Questions and Answers to the Orthodox]*; Tho[mas] Bartholinus, *Esu Sanguinis.*
¶ xv *Acts*, 20, 29.

of Peter Martyr, Zanchy, Aretius, Jac. Capellus, Hiddiger, Cocceius, Bochartus, &c. amongst the protestants; and *instar omnium*, by Salmasius, Grotius, Vossius, Blundel: in a word, by the learn'd of both persuasions, favourable enough to these opinions, Cajetan and Calvin only excepted, who hold, that as to abstinence from flesh, there was no positive command or imposition concerning it; but that the use of herbs and fruit was recommended rather for temperance sake, and the prolongation of life: upon which score I am inclin'd to believe that the ancient THERAPENTAI [*RECTE* THERAPEUTAI, SERVANTS OF A RELIGIOUS SECT], and other devout and contemplative sects, distinguish'd themselves; whose course of life we have at large describ'd in *Philo (who liv'd and taught much in gardens) with others of the abstemious Christians; among whom, Clemens brings in St. Mark the Evangelist himself, James our Lord's brother, St. John, &c. and with several of the devout sex, the famous diaconesse Olympias, mention'd by Palladius (not to name the rest) who abstaining from flesh, betook themselves to herbs and sallets upon the account of temperance, and the vertues accompanying it; and concerning which the incomparable Grotius declares ingenuously his opinion to be far from censuring, not only those who forbear the eating flesh and blood, *experimenti causa*, and for discipline sake; but such as forbear *ex opinione*, (because it has been the ancient custom) provided they blam'd none who freely us'd their liberty; and I think he's in the right.

But leaving this controversie (*nè nimium extra oleas*) it has often been objected, that fruit, and plants, and all other things, may since the beginning, and as the world grows older, have universally become effœte, impair'd and divested of those nutritious and transcendent vertues they were at first endow'd withal: but as this is begging the

---

* Philo , *De Vit[a] Contemp[lativa]*; Joseph[us], *Antiq[uitates Iudaicae]*, Lib.13, Cap.9.

question, and to which we have already spoken; so all are not agreed that there is any, the least *decay in nature, where equal industry and skill's apply'd. 'Tis true indeed, that the *Ordo Foliatorum,* Feuill-antines (a late order of ascetic nuns) amongst other mortifications, made trial upon the leaves of plants alone, to which they would needs confine themselves; but were not able to go through that thin and meagre diet: but then it would be enquir'd whether they had not first, and from their very childhood, been fed and brought up with flesh, and better sustenance till they enter'd the cloyster; and what the vegetables and the preparation of them were allow'd by their institut-ion? Wherefore this is nothing to our modern use of sallets, or its dis-paragement. In the mean time, that we still think it not only possible, but likely, and with no great art or charge (taking roots and fruit into the basket) substantially to maintain mens lives in health and vigour: for to this, and less than this, we have the suffrage of the great ¶Hippocrates himself; who thinks, *ab initio etiam hominum* (as well as other animals) *tali victu usum esse,* and needed no other food. Nor is it an inconsiderable speculation, that since all flesh is grass (not in a figurative, but natural and real sense) man himself, who lives on flesh, and I think upon no earthly animal whatsoever, but such as feed on grass, is nourish'd with them still; and so becoming an incarnate herb, and innocent canibal, may truly be said to devour himself.

We have said nothing of the Lotophagi, and such as (like St. John the Baptist, and other religious ascetics) were feeders on the summities and tops of plants: but as divers of those, and others we have mention'd, were much in times of streights, persecutions, and other circumstances, which did not in the least make it a pretence, exempting them from labour, and other humane offices, by ensnaring obligations and vows (never to be useful to the publick, in whatever

---

* Hackwell [George Hakewill], *Apolog[ie...of the Power and Providence of God].*
¶ Hippoc[rates], *De Vetere Medicina,* Cap. 6, 7.

exigency) so I cannot but take notice of what a learned *critic speaking of mens neglecting plain and essential duties, under colour of exercising themselves in a more sublime course of piety, and being righteous above what is commanded (as those who seclude themselves in monasteries) that they manifestly discover excessive pride, hatred of their neighbour, impatience of injuries; to which add, melancholy plots and machinations; and that he must be either stupid, or infected with the same vice himself, who admires this ETHELOPERIA-GOTHRESKEIA [VOLUNTARY SEEKERS OF RELIGION], or thinks they were for that cause the more pleasing to God. This being so, what may we then think of such armies of hermits, monks and friers, who pretending to justifie a mistaken zeal and meritorious abstinence; not only by a peculiar diet and distinction of meats (which God without distinction has made the moderate use of common and ¶indifferent amongst Christians) but by other sordid usages, and unnecessary hardships, wilfully prejudice their health and constitution? and through a singular manner of living, dark and saturnine; whilst they would seem to abdicate and forsake the world (in imitation, as they pretend, of the ancient eremites) take care to settle, and build their warm and stately nests in the most populous cities, and places of resort; ambitious doubtless of the peoples veneration and opinion of an extraordinary sanctity; and therefore flying the desarts, where there is indeed no use of them; and flocking to the towns and cities where there is less, indeed none at all; and therefore no marvel that the Emperour Valentinian banished them the cities, and Constantine Copronymus finding them seditious, oblig'd them to marry, to leave their cells, and live as did others. For of these, some there are who seldom speak, and therefore edifie none; sleep little and lie hard, are clad nastily, and eat meanly (and oftentimes that which is

---

* L.C. *Annot. in Coloss[ians]*, c[ap]. 2.
¶ 2 Timothy, iv. 3.

unwholsom) and therefore benefit none: not because they might not, both for their own, and the good of others, and the publick; but because they will not; custom, and a prodigious *sloth accompanying it; which renders it so far from penance, and the mortification pretended, that they know not how to live, or spend their time otherwise. This, as I have often consider'd, so was I glad to find it justly perstring'd, and taken notice of by a ¶learned person, amongst others of his useful remarks abroad.

'These, says he, willingly renouncing the innocent comforts of life, plainly shew it to proceed more from a chagrin and morose humour, than from any true and serious principle of sound religion; which teaches men to be useful in their generations, sociable and communicative, unaffected, and by no means singular and fantastic in garb and habit, as are these (forsooth) fathers (as they affect to be call'd)' spending their days in idle and fruitless forms, and tedious repetitions; and thereby thinking to merit the reward of those ancient, and truly pious solitaries, who, God knows, were driven from their countries and repose, by the incursions of barbarous nations (whilst these have no such cause) and compell'd to austerities, not of their own chusing and making, but the publick calamity; and to labour with their hands for their own, and others necessary support, as well as with their prayers and holy lives, examples to all the world: and some of these indeed (besides the solitaries of the Thebaid, who wrought for abundance of poor Christians, sick, and in captivity) I might bring in, as such who deserv'd to have their names preserv'd; not for their rigorous fare, and uncouth disguises; but for teaching that the grace

---

* This, with their prodigious ignorance, see Mab[illon, *Traité] des études monastiques*, Part 2, c[ap]. 17.

¶ Dr. Lister's *Journey to Paris*. See *L'Apocalyps de Meliton, ou Revelation des Mysteres Cenobitiques.*

of temperance and other vertues, consisted in a cheerful, innocent, and profitable conversation.

And now to recapitulate what other prerogatives the hortulan provision has been celebrated for, besides its antiquity, health and longævity of the antediluvians; that temperance, frugality, leisure, ease, and innumerable other vertues and advantages, which accompany it, are no less attributable to it. Let us hear our excellent botanist *Mr Ray.

'The use of plants (says he) is all our life long of that universal importance and concern that we can neither live nor subsist in any plenty with decency, or conveniency or be said to live indeed at all without them: whatsoever food is necessary to sustain us, whatsoever contributes to delight and refresh us, are supply'd and brought forth out of that plentiful and abundant store: and ah, how much more innocent, sweet and healthful, is a table cover'd with these, than with all the reeking flesh of butcher'd and slaughter'd animals! Certainly man by nature was never made to be a carnivorous creature; nor is he arm'd at all for prey and rapin, with gag'd and pointed teeth and crooked claws, sharpned to rend and tear: but with gentle hands to gather fruit and vegetables, and with teeth to chew and eat them: nor do we so much as read the use of flesh for food, was at all permitted him, 'till after the universal deluge, &c.'

To this might we add that transporting consideration, becoming both our veneration and admiration of the infinitely wise and glorious

---

* *Plantarum usus latissimè patet, & in omni vitæ parte occurrit, sine illis lautè, sine illis commodè non vivitur, ac nec vivitur omninò. Quæcunque ad victu necessaria sunt, quæcunque ad delicias faciunt, è locupletissimo suo penu abundè subministrant: Quantò ex eis mensa innocentior, mundior, salubrior, quam ex animalium cæde & Laniena! Homo certè naturâ animal carnivorum non est; nullis ad prædam & rapinam armis instructum; non dentibus exertis & serratis, non unguibus aduncis: Manus ad fructos colligendos, dentes ad mandendos comparati; nec legimus se ante diluvium carnes ad esum concessas, &c.* Raii [John Ray], *Hist[oria] Plan[tarum]*, Lib. I, Cap. 24.

Author of Nature, who has given to plants such astonishing properties; such fiery heat in some to warm and cherish, such coolness in others to temper and refresh, such pinguid juice to nourish and feed the body, such quickening acids to compel the appetite, and grateful vehicles to court the obedience of the palate, such vigour to renew and support our natural strength, such ravishing flavour and perfumes to recreate and delight us: in short, such spirituous and active force to animate and revive every faculty and part, to all the kinds of human, and, I had almost said heavenly capacity too. What shall we add more? Our gardens present us with them all; and whilst the shambles are cover'd with gore and stench, our sallets scape the insults of the summer fly, purifies and warms and blood against winter rage: nor wants there variety in more abundance, than any of the former ages could shew.

Survey we their bills of fare, and numbers of courses serv'd up by Athenæus, drest with all the garnish of Nicander and other Grecian wits: what has the Roman grand sallet worth the naming? *Parat convivium*, the guests are nam'd indeed, and we are told,

> ———*Varias, quas habet hortus opes?*
> How richly the Garden's stor'd!

> *In quibus est Luctuca sedens, & tonsile porrum,*
> *Nec deest ructatrix Mentha, nec herba salax, &c.*

A Goodly Sallet!

Lettuce, leeks, mint, rocket, colewort-tops, with oyl and eggs, and such an hotch-pot following (as the cook in Plautus would deservedly laugh at) but how infinitely out-done in this age of ours, by the variety of so many rare edules unknown to the ancients, that there's no room for the comparison. And, for magnificence, let the sallet drest by the

---

* Mart[ial], lib. x, Epig[ram] 44.

lady for an entertainment made by Jacobus Catsius (describ'd by the poet *Barlæus) shew; not at all yet out-doing what we every day almost find at our Lord Mayor's table, and other great persons, lovers of the gardens; that sort of elegant cookery being capable of such wonderful variety, tho' not altogether wanting of old, if that be true which is related to us of ¶Nicomedes a certain King of Bithynia, whose cook made him a pilchard (a fish he exceedingly long'd for) of a well dissembl'd turnip, carv'd in its shape, and drest with oyl, salt, and pepper, that so deceiv'd, and yet pleased the prince, that he commended it for the best fish he had ever eaten. Nor does all this exceed what every industrious gardiner may innocently enjoy, as well as the greatest potentate on earth.

> Vitellius his Table, to which every Day
> All Courtiers did a constant Tribute pay,
> Could nothing more delicious afford
> Than Nature's Liberality.
> Help'd with a little Art and Industry,
> Allows the meanest Gard'ners Board,
> The wanton Taste no Fish or Fowl can chuse,
> For which the Grape or Melon she would lose.
> Tho' all th' Inhabitants of Sea and Air,
> Be listed in the Glutton's Bill of Fare;
> Yet still the Sallet, and the Fruit we see
> Plac'd the third Story high in all her Luxury.

So the sweet §poet, whom I can never part with for his love to this delicious toil, and the honour he has done me.

Verily, the infinite plenty and abundance, with which the benign

---

* Barl[æus], *Eleg[y]*, lib. 3.
¶ Athen[æus], *Deip[nosphistæ]*, l[ib]. I.
§ Cowley, *Garden*, Stanz[a] 6.

and bountiful author of nature has stor'd the whole terrestrial world, more with plants and vegetables than with any other provision whatsoever; and the variety not only equal, but by far exceeding the pleasure and delight of taste (above all the art of the kitchen, than ever *Apicius knew) seems loudly to call, and kindly invite all her living inhabitants (none excepted) who are of gentle nature, and most useful, to the same hospitable and common-board, which first she furnished with plants and fruit, as to their natural and genuine pasture; nay, and of the most wild, and savage too *ab origine*: as in paradise, where, as the evangelical ¶prophet adumbrating the future glory of the catholick church, (of which that happy garden was the antitype) the wolf and the lamb, the angry and furious lion, should eat grass and herbs together with the ox. But after all, *latet anguis in herba*, there's a snake in the grass; luxury and excess in our most innocent fruitions. There was a time indeed when the garden furnish'd entertainments for the most renown'd heroes, virtuous and excellent persons; till the blood-thirsty and ambitious, over-running the nations, and by murders and rapine rifl'd the world, to transplant its luxury to its new mistriss, Rome. Those whom heretofore §two acres of land would have satisfied, and plentifully maintain'd; had afterwards their very kitchens almost as large as their first territories: nor was that enough: entire †forests and parks, warrens and fish-ponds, and ample lakes to furnish their tables, so as men could not

---

* Hence in Macrobius, *Sat[urnalia]*, lib. vii, c[ap]. 5, we find Eupolis the Comedian in his *Æges*, bringing in goats boasting the variety of their food, BOSKOMETH' HULES APO PANTODAPES, ELATES [WE GRAZE ON ALL SORTS OF TREES, FIR] &c. After which follows a Banquet of innumerable sorts

¶ Esa [Isaiah], lxv, 25.

§ *Bina tunc jugera populo Romano satis erat, nullique majorem modum attribuit, quo servos paulo ante principis Neronis, contemptis hujus spatii Viridariis, piscinas juvat habere majores, gratúmque, si non aliquem & culinas.* Plin[y], *Hist. Nat. [Naturalis Historia]*, lib. xviii, c[ap]. 2.

† *Interea gustus elementa per omnia quærunt.* Juv[enal], Sat[ire] 4.

live by one another without oppression: nay, and to shew how the best, and most innocent things may be perverted; they chang'd those frugal and *inemptas dapes* of their ancestors, to that height and profusion that we read of *edicts and sumptuary laws, enacted to restrain even the pride and excess of sallets. But so it was not when the pease-field spread a table for the conquerors of the world, and their grounds were cultivated *vomere laureato, & triumphali aratore*: The greatest princes took the spade and the plough-staff in the same hand they held the sceptre; and the noblest ¶families thought it no dishonour, to derive their names from plants and sallet-herbs: they arriv'd, I say to that pitch of ingrossing all that was but green, and could be vary'd by the cook (*Heu quam prodiga ventris!*) that, as Pliny tells us (*non sine pudore*, not without blushing) a poor man could hardly find a thistle to dress for his supper; or what his hungry §ass would not touch, for fear of pricking his lips.

Verily the luxury of the East ruin'd the greatest monarchies; first, the Persian, then the Grecian, and afterwards Rome her self: by what steps, see elegantly describ'd in old †Gratius the Faliscian, deploring his own age compar'd with the former:

---

* Cicero, *Epist[ulae]*, Lib. 7, Ep. 26. Complaining of a costly Sallet, that had almost cost him his life.

¶ Valeriana, *that of* Lectucini, Achilleia, Lysimachia. *Fabius, Cicero, Lentulus, Piso, &c. à Fabis, Cicere, Lente, Pisis bene serendis dicti,* Plin[y].

§ *Mirum esset non licere pecori Carduis vesci, non licet plebei, &c.* And in another place, *Quoniam portenta quoque terrarum in ganeam vertimus, etiam quæ refugeant quadrupedes consciæ,* Plin[y], *Hist. Nat. [Naturalis Historia],* l[ib]. xix, c[ap]. 8.

† Gra[tius] Falisc[us], *Cyneget[ica]*, [in Christopher] Was[e]. See concerning this excess, Macr[obius], *Sat[urnalia]*, l[ib]. 2, c[ap]. 9. & sequ.

O quantum, & quoties decoris frustrata paterni!
At qualis nostris, quam simplex mensa Camillis!
Qui tibi cultus erat post tot, serrane, triumphos?
Ergo illi ex habitu, virtutisq; indole priscæ,
Imposuere orbi Romam caput:—

Neighb'ring Excesses being made thine own,
How art thou fall'n from thine old Renown!
But our Camilli did but plainly fare,
No Port did oft triumphant Serran bear:
Therefore such Hardship, and their Heart so great
Gave Rome to be the World's Imperial Seat.

But as these were the sensual and voluptuous, who abus'd their plenty, spent their fortunes and shortned their lives by their debauches; so never did they taste the delicaces, and true satisfaction of a sober repast, and the infinite conveniences of what well-stor'd garden affords; so elegantly describ'd by the *Naturalist, as costing neither fuel nor fire to boil, pains or time to gather and prepare, *Res expedita & parata semper*: All was so near at hand, readily drest, and of so easie digestion; as neither to offend the brain, or dull the senses; and in the greatest dearth of corn, a little bread suffic'd. In all events,

¶*Panis ematur, Olus, Vini Sextarius adde*
Queis humana sibi doleat natura negatis.

Bread, Wine, and wholsome Sallets you may buy,
What Nature adds besides is Luxury.

---

* *Horti maximè placebant, quia non egerent igni, parceréntque ligno, expedita rès, & parata semper, unde Acetaria appellantur, facilia concoqui, nec oneratura sensum cibo, & quæ minimè accenderent desiderium panis.* Plin[y], *Hist. Nat. [Naturalis Historia]*, Lib. xix, c.4. And of this exceeding frugality of the Romans, till after the Mithridatic War, see Athenæus *Deip[nosophistæ]*, Lib. 6, cap. 21.
¶ Horat. [Horace], *Serm[ones (Satires)]*, Sat. I.

They could then make an honest meal, and dine upon a sallet, without so much as a grain of exotic spice; and the potagere was in such reputation, that she who neglected her kitchen-garden (for that was still the good woman's province) was never reputed a tolerable huswife: *si vespertinus subitò te oppresserit hospes*, she was never surpriz'd, had all (as we said) at hand, and could in a trice set forth an handsome sallet: and if this was happiness, *convictus facilis sine arte mensa* (as the poet reckons) it was here in perfection. In a word, so universal was the sallet, that the *un-bloody shambles (as Pliny calls them) yielded the ¶Roman state a more considerable custom (when there was little more than honest cabbage and worts) than almost any thing besides brought to market.

They spent not then so much precious time as afterwards they did, gorging themselves with flesh and fish, so as hardly able to rise, without reeking and reeling from table.

> §———*Vides ut pallidus omnis*
> *Cæna desurgat dubia? quin corpus onustum*
> *Hesternis vitiis, animum quoque prægravat unà,*
> *Atque assigit humo divinæ particulam auræ.*

> See but how pale they look, how wretchedly,
> With Yesterday's Surcharge disturb'd they be!
> Nor Body only suff'ring, but the Mind,
> That Nobler Part, dull'd and depress'd we find.

Drowsie and unapt for business, and other nobler parts of life.

---

* *Nequam esse in domo matrem familias (etenim hæc cura Fœminæ dicebatur) ubi indiligens esset hortus.*

¶ *Alterum succidium.* Cic[ero] in *Catone [Cato maior].* Tiberias had a tribute of skirrits paid him.

§ Hor[ace], *Sat[ires],* l[ib]. 2. *Vix præ vino sustinet palpebras, eunti in consilium, &c.* See the oration of C. Titius de Leg. Fan.[,] Mac[robius], *Sat[urnalia],* l[ib].2, c[ap]. 12.

Time was before men in those golden days: their spirits were brisk and lively.

> —*Ubi dicto citius curata sopori*
> *Membra dedit, Vegetus præscripta ad munera surgit.*

With shorter, but much sweeter Sleep content,
Vigorous and fresh, about their Business went.

And men had their wits about them; their appetites were natural, their sleep *molli sub arbore*, sound, sweet and kindly: that excellent Emperour Tacitus being us'd to say of lettuce, that he did *somnum se mercari* when he eat of them, and call'd it a sumptuous feast, with a sallet and a single pullet, which was usually all the flesh-meat that sober prince eat of; whilst Maximinus (a profess'd enemy to sallet) is reported to have scarce been satisfied, with sixty pounds of flesh, and drink proportionable.

There was then also far less expensive grandure, but far more true state; which consuls, great statemen (and such as atchiev'd the most renown'd actions) sup'd in their garden; not under costly, gilded, and inlaid roofs, but the spreading platan; and drank of the chrystal brook, and by temperance, and healthy frugality, maintain'd the glory of sallets, *Ah quanto innocentiore victu!* with what content and satisfaction! Nor, as we said, wanted there variety; for so in the most blissful place, and innocent state of nature, see how the first empress of the world regal's her celestial guest:

> *With sav'ry Fruit of Taste to Please
> True Appetite, ——— and brings
> Whatever Earth's all-bearing Mother yields
> ——— Fruit of all kinds, in Coat
> Rough, or smooth-Rind, or bearded Husk, or Shell.

---

* Milton's *Paradise [Lost]*, l[ib].v, ver. 228. [This is a composite quotation from ll. 305-345 of Bk. 5 of *Paradise Lost*.]

Heaps with unsparing Hand: For Drink the Grape
She crushes, innoffensive Moust, and Meathes
From many a Berry, and from sweet Kernel prest,
She temper'd dulcid Creams.—

Then for the board.

—Rais'd of a grassy Turf
The Table was, and Mossy Seats had round;
And on the ample Square from Side to Side,
All Autumn pil'd: Ah Innocence,
Deserving Paradise!

Thus, the hortulan provision of the *golden age fitted all places, times and persons; and when man is restor'd to that state again, it will be as it was in the beginning.

But now after all (and for close of all) let none yet imagine, that whilst we justifie our present subject through all the topics of panegyric, we would in favour of the sallet, drest with all its pomp and advantage turn mankind to grass again; which were ungratefully to neglect the bounty of heaven, as well as his health and comfort: but by these noble instances and examples, to reproach the luxury of the present age; and by shewing the infinite blessing and effects of temperance, and the vertues accompanying it; with how little nature, and a ¶civil appetite may be happy, contented with moderate things, and within a little compass, reserving the rest, to the nobler parts of life. And thus of old,

Hoc erat in votis, modus agri non
ita magnus, &c.

---

* At victus illa ætas cui fecimus aurea nomen
  Fructibus arboreis, & quas humus educat herbis
  Fortunata fuit. —— Met[amorphoses], xv.
¶ Bene moratus venter.

He that was possess'd of a little spot of ground, and well-cultivated garden, with other moderate circumstances, had *hæredium*. All that a modest man could well desire. Then,

> ¶Happy the Man, who from Ambition freed,
> A little Garden, little Field does feed.
> The Field gives frugal Nature what's requir'd;
> The Garden what's luxuriously desir'd:
> The specious Evils of an anxious Life,
> He leaves to Fools to be their endless Strife.

> *O Fortunatos nimium bona si sua norint*
> *Horticulos!*

---

* TAB.II. [This reference is obscure, it is omitted in the 1825 edition of Evelyn's Miscellaneous Writings.]
¶ *Fœlix, quem miserâ procul ambitione remotum*
    Parvus ager placidè, parvus & hortus, alit.
  Præbet ager quicquid frugi natura requirit,
    Hortus habet quicquid luxuriosa petit,
  Cætera sollicitæ speciosa incommoda vitæ
    Permittit stultis quærere, habere malis.
  Cowley, *Plant[arum]*, lib. iv.

FINIS.

APPENDIX.

T HO' it was far from our first intention to charge this small volume and discourse concerning crude sallets, with any of the following receits: yet having since received them from an experienc'd housewife; and that they may possibly be useful to correct, preserve and improve our *Acetaria*, we have allow'd them place as an appendant variety upon occasion: nor account we it the least dishonour to our former treatise, that we kindly entertain'd them; since (besides divers learned physicians, and such as have *ex professo* written *de re cibaria*) we have the examples of many other ¶noble and illustrious persons, both among the ancient and modern.

Artichoak. Clear it of the leaves and cut the bottoms in pretty thin slices or quarters; then fry them in fresh butter and some parsley, till it is crisp, and the slices tender; and so dish them with other fresh melted butter.

How a poiverade is made, and the bottoms preserv'd all the winter, See *Acetaria.* p. 18.

Ashen-keys. *See* Pickle.

Asparagus. *See* Pickle.

Beets.
Broom.
Buds.
Capers. } *See* Pickle.

Carrot. *See* Pudding.

Champignon. *See* Mushroom.

¶ Plin[y], Athenæus, Macrobius, Bacon, Boyle, Digby, &c.

2. *Chessnut.* Roasted under the embers, or dry fryed, till they shell, and quit their husks, may be slit; the juice of orange squeezed on a lump of hard sugar dissolv'd; to which add some claret wine.

Collyflower.
Cucumber.
Elder-flowers. } See Pickle.
Flowers.
Gilly-flowers.

Herbs. *See* Pudding *and* Tart.
Limon. *See* Pickle.

3. *Mushroom.* Chuse the small, firm and white buttons, growing upon sweet pasture grounds, neither under, or about any trees: strip off the upper skin, and pare away all the black spungy bottom part; then slice them in quarters, and cast them in water a while to cleanse: then boil them in fresh water, and a little sweet butter; (some boil them a quarter of an hour first) and then taking them out, dry them in a cloth, pressing out the water, and whilst hot, add the butter; and then boiling a full hour (to exhaust the malignity) shift them in another clean water, with butter, as before till they become sufficiently tender. Then being taken out, pour upon them as much strong mutton (or other) broth as will cover them, with six spoonfuls of white-wine, twelve cloves, as many pepper-corns, four small young onions, half an handful of persly bound up with two or three spriggs of thyme, an anchovy, oysters raw, or pickl'd; a little salt, sweet butter; and so let them stew. See *Acetar.* p. 30.

Another.
Prepar'd, and cleans'd as above, and cast into fountain-water, to preserve them from growing black; boil them in fresh water and salt; and whilst on the fire, cast in the mushrooms, letting them boil till

they become tender: then stew them leisurely between two dishes (the water being drained from them) in a third part of white-wine and butter, a small bundle of sweet herbs at discretion. To these add broth as before, with cloves, mace, nutmeg, anchovies (one is sufficient) oysters, &c. a small onion, with the green stem chopt small; and lastly, some mutton-gravy, rubbing the dish gently with a clove of garlick, or some rocombo seeds in its stead. Some beat the yolk of a fresh egg with vinegar, and butter, and a little pepper.

In France some (more compendiously being peel'd and prepared) cast them into a pipkin, where, with the sweet herbs, spice, and an onion they stew them in their own juice, without any other water or liquor at all; and then taking out the herbs and onion, thicken it with a little butter, and so eat them.

In poiverade.

The large mushrooms well cleansed, &c. being cut into quarters and strewed with pepper and salt, are broil'd on the grid-iron, and eaten with fresh butter.

In powder.

Being fresh gathered, cleans'd, &c. and cut in pieces, stew them in water and salt; and being taken forth, dry them with a cloth: then putting them into an earth-glazed pot, set them into the oven after the bread is drawn: repeat this till they are perfectly dry; and reserve them in papers to crumble into what sauce you please. For the rest, see Pickle.

4. *Mustard.* Procure the best and weightiest seed: cast it into water two or three times, till no more of the husk arise: then taking out the sound (which will sink to the bottom) rub it very dry in warm course cloths, shewing it also a little to the fire in a dish or pan. Then stamp it as small as to pass through a fine tiffany sieve: then slice

some horse-radish, and lay it to soak in strong vinegar, with a small lump of hard sugar (which some leave out) to temper the flower with, being drained from the radish, and so pot it all in a glaz'd mug, with an onion, and keep it well stop'd with a cork upon a bladder, which is the more cleanly: but this receit is improv'd, if instead of vinegar, water only, or the broth of powder'd beef be made use of. And to some of this mustard adding verjuice, sugar, claret-wine, and juice of limon, you have an excellent sauce in any sort of flesh or fish.

Note, that a pint of good seed is enough to make at one time, and to keep fresh a competent while. What part of it does not pass the sarse, may be beaten again; and you may reserve the flower in a well closed glass, and make fresh mustard when you please. See *Acetaria*, p. 38, 56.

Nasturtium. *Vide* Pickle.

Orange. *See* Limon in Pickle.

5. *Parsnip*. Take the large roots, boil them, and strip the skin: then slit them long-ways into pretty thin slices; flower and fry them in fresh butter till they look brown. The sauce is other sweet butter melted. Some strow sugar and cinamon upon them. Thus you may accommodate other roots.

There is made a mash or pomate of this root, being boiled very tender with a little fresh cream; and being heated again, put to it some butter, a little sugar and juice of limon; dish it upon sippets; sometimes a few Corinths are added.

Peny-royal. *See* Pudding.

Pickles.

6. Pickled *Artichoaks*. See *Acetaria*, p. 18.

7. *Ashen-keys* Gather them young, and boil them in three or four waters to extract the bitterness; and when they feel tender, prepare a syrup of sharp white-wine vinegar, sugar, and a little water. Then boil them on a very quick fire, and they will become of a green colour, fit to be potted so soon as cold.

8. *Asparagus.* Break off the hard ends and put them in white-wine vinegar and salt, well covered with it; and so let them remain for six weeks: then taking them out, boil the liquour or pickle, and scum it carefully. If need be, renew the vinegar and salt; and when 'tis cold, pot them up again. Thus may one keep them the whole year.

9. *Beans.* Take such as are fresh young, and approaching their full growth. Put them into a strong brine of white-wine vinegar and salt able to bear an egg. Cover them very close, and so will they be preserved twelve months: but a month before you use them, take our what quantity you think sufficient for your spending a quarter of a year (for so long the second pickle will keep them sound) and boil them in a skillet of fresh water, till they begin to look green, as they soon will do. Then placing them one by one, (to drain upon a clean course napkin) range them row by row in a jarr, and cover them with vinegar, and what spice you please; some weight being laid upon them to keep them under the pickle. Thus you may preserve French beans, harico's, &c. the whole year about.

10. *Broom-buds* and *pods.* Make a strong pickle, as above; stir it very well, till the salt be quite dissolved, clearing off the dregs and scum. The next day pour it from the bottom; and having rubbed the buds dry pot them in a pickle-glass, which should be frequently

shaken, till they sink under it, and keep it will stopt and covered.

Thus may you pickle any other buds. Or as follows:

11. Of *elder*.   Take the largest buds, and boil them in a skillet with salt and water, sufficient only to scald them; and so (being taken off the fire) let them remain covered till green; and then pot them with vinegar and salt, which has had one boil up to cleanse it.

12. *Collyflowers*.   Boil them till they fall in pieces: then with some of the stalk, and worst of the flower, boil it in a part of the liquor till pretty strong: then being taken off, strain it; and when settled, clear it from the bottom. Then with dill, gross pepper, a pretty quantity of salt, when cold, add as much vinegar as will make it sharp, and pour all upon the collyflower; and so as to keep them from touching one another; which is prevented by putting paper close to them.

Cornelians are pickled like olives.

13. *Cowslips*.   Pickt very clean; to each pound of flowers allow about one pound of loaf-sugar, and one pint of white-wine vinegar, which boil to a syrup, and cover it scalding-hot. Thus you may pickle clove-gillyflowers, elder, and other flowers, which being eaten alone, make a very agreeable salletine.

14. *Cucumbers*.   Take the gorkems, or smaller cucumbers; put them into rape-vinegar, and boyl, and cover them so close, as none of the vapour may issue forth; and also let them stand till the next day: then boil them in fresh white-wine vinegar, with large mace, nutmeg, ginger, white pepper, and a little salt, (according to discretion) straining the former liquor from the cucumbers; and so place them in a jarr, or wide mouthed glass, laying a little dill and fennel between each rank; and covering all with the fresh scalding-hot pickle, keep all close, and repeat it daily, till you find them sufficiently green. *[Note the amendment in the errata on p. 14.]*

In the same sort cucumbers of the largest size, being peel'd and cut into thin slices, are very delicate.

Another.

Wiping them clean, put them in a very strong brine of water and salt, to soak two or three hours or longer, if you see cause: then range them in the jarr or barrellet with herbs and spice as usual; and cover them with hot liquor made of two parts beer-vinegar, and one of white-wine vinegar: let all be very well closed. A fortnight after scald the pickle again, and repeat it, as above: thus they will keep longer, and from being so soon sharp, eat crimp and well tasted, tho' not altogether so green. You may add a walnut-leaf, hysop, costmary, &c. and as some do, strow on them a little powder of roch-allom, which makes them firm and eatable within a month or six weeks after.

Mango of Cucumbers

Take the biggest cucumbers (and most of the mango size) that look green: open them on the top or side; and scooping out the seeds, supply their place with a small clove of garlick, or some roccombo seeds. Then put them into an earthen glazed jarr, or wide-mouth'd glass, with as much white wine vinegar as will cover them. Boil them in the vinegar with pepper, cloves, mace, &c. and when off the fire, as much salt as will make a gentle brine; and so pour all boyling hot on the cucumbers, covering them close till the next day. Then put them with a little dill, and pickle into a large skillet; and giving them a boyl or two, return them into the vessel again: and when all is cold add a good spoonful of the best mustard, keeping it from the air, and so have you an excellent mango. When you have occasion to take any out, make use of a spoon, and not your fingers.

Elder. *See* Buds.

Flowers. *See* Cowslips, and for other Flowers.

15. *Limon.*   Take slices of the thick rind limon, boil and shift them in several waters, till they are pretty tender: then drain and wipe them dry with a clean cloth; and make a pickle with a little white-wine vinegar, one part to two of fair water, and a little sugar, carefully scum'd. When all is cold, pour it on the peel'd rind, and cover it all close in a convenient glass jarr. Some make a syrup of vinegar, white-wine and sugar not too thick, and pour it on hot.

16. *Melon.*   The abortive and after-fruit of melons being pickled as cucumber, make an excellent sallet.

17. *Mushrom.*   Take a quart of the best white-wine vinegar; as much of white-wine, cloves, mace, nutmeg a pretty quantity, beaten together: let the spice boil therein to the consumption of half; then taken off, and being cold pour the liquour on the mushroms; but leave out the boiled spice, and cast in of the same sort of spice whole, the nutmeg only slit in quarters, with some limon-peel, white pepper; and if you please a whole raw onion, which take out again when it begins to perish.

Another.

The mushroms peel'd, &c. throw them into water, and then a sauce-pan, with some long pepper, cloves, mace, a quarter'd nutmeg, with an onion, shallot, or roccombo-seed, and a little salt. Let them all boil a quarter of an hour on a very quick fire: then take out and cold, with a pretty quantity of the former spice, boil them in some white-wine; which (being cold) cast upon the mushroms, and fill up the pot with the best white-wine, a bay-leaf or two, and an handful of salt: then cover them with the liquour; and if for long keeping, pour sallet-oil over all, tho' they will be preserved a year without it.

They are sometimes boil'd in salt and water, with some milk, and laying them in the colender to drain, till cold, and wiped dry, cast them into the pickle with the white wine, vinegar and salt, grated nutmeg, ginger bruised, cloves, mace, white pepper and limon peel; pour the liquor on them cold without boiling.

18. *Nasturtium Indicum.* Gather the buds before they open to flower; lay them in the shade three or four hours, and putting them into an earthen glazed vessel, pour good vinegar on them, and cover it with a board. Thus letting it stand for eight or ten days: then being taken out, and gently press'd, cast them into fresh vinegar, and let them so remain as long as before. Repeat this a third time, and barrel them up with vinegar and a little salt.

Orange. *See* Limon.

20. *Potato.* The small green fruit (when about the size of the wild cherry) being pickled, is an agreeable sallet. But the root being roasted under the embers, or otherwise, open'd with a knife, the pulp is butter'd in the skin, of which it will take up a good quantity, and is seasoned with a little salt and pepper. Some eat them with sugar together in the skin, which has a pleasant crimpness. They are also stew'd and bak'd in pyes, &c.

21. *Purselan.* Lay the stalks in an earthen pan; then cover them with beer-vinegar and water, keeping them down with a competent weight to imbibe, three days: being taken out, put them into a pot with as much white-wine vinegar as will cover them again; and close the lid with paste to keep in the steam: then set them on the fire for three or four hours, often shaking and stirring them: then open the cover, and turn and remove those stalks which lie at the bottom, to the top, and boil them as before, till they are all of a colour. When all is cold, put them with fresh white-wine vinegar, and so you may preserve them the whole year round.

20. *Radish.*   The seed-pods of this root being pickl'd, are a pretty sallet.

23. *Sampier.*   Let it be gathered about Michaelmas (or the spring) and put two or three hours into a brine of water and salt; then into a clean tin'd brass pot, with three parts of strong white-wine vinegar, and one part of water and salt, or as much as will cover the sampier, keeping the vapour from issuing out, by pasting down the pot-lid, and so hang it over the fire for half an hour only. Being taken off, let it remain cover'd till it be cold; and then put it up into small barrels or jars, with the liquor, and some fresh vinegar, water and salt; and thus it will keep very green. If you be near the sea, that water will supply the place of brine. This is the Dover receit.

24. *Walnuts.*   Gather the nuts young, before they begin to harden, but not before the kernel is pretty white: steep them in as much water as will more then cover them. Then set them on the fire, and when the water boils, and grows black, pour it off, and supply it with fresh, boiling it as before, and continuing to shift it till it become clear, and the nuts pretty tender: then let them be put into clean spring-water for two days, changing it as before, with fresh, two or three times within this space: then lay them to drain, and dry on a clean course cloth, and put them up in a glass jar, with a few walnut leaves, dill, cloves, pepper, whole mace and salt; strowing them under every layer of nuts, till the vessel be three quarters full; and lastly, replenishing it with the best vinegar, keep it well covered; and so they will be fit to spend within three months.

To make a mango with them.

The green nuts prepared as before, cover the bottom of the jar with some dill, an handful of bay-salt, &c. and then a bed of nuts; and so stratum upon stratum, as above, adding to the spice some roccombo-seeds; and filling the rest of the jar with the best white-wine vinegar, mingled with the best mustard; and so let them remain close covered, during two or three months time: and thus have you a more agreeable mango than what is brought us from abroad; which you may use in any sauce, and is of it self a rich condiment.

Thus far *Pickles*.

25. *Potage Maigre.* Take four quarts of spring-water, two or three onions stuck with some cloves, two or three slices of limon-peel, salt, whole white pepper, mace, a raze or two of ginger, tied up in a fine cloth (lawn or tiffany) and make all boil for half an hour; then having spinage, sorrel, white beet-chard, a little cabbage, a few small tops of cives, wash'd and pick'd clean, shred them well, and cast them into the liquor, with a pint of blue pease boil'd soft and strain'd, with a bunch of sweet herbs, the top and bottom of a French roll; and so suffer it to boil during three hours; and then dish it with another small French roll, and slices about the dish: some cut bread in slices, and frying them brown (being dried) put them into the pottage just as it is going to be eaten.

The same herbs, clean wash'd, broken and pulled asunder only, being put in a close cover'd pipkin, without any other water or liquor, will stew in their own juice and moisture. Some add an whole onion, which after a while should be taken out, remembring to season it with salt and spice, and serve it up with bread and a piece of fresh butter.

26. *Pudding of carrot.* Pare off some of the crust of manchet-bread, and grate off half as much of the rest as there is of the root, which must also be grated: then take half a pint of fresh cream or new milk, half a pound of fresh butter, fix new laid eggs (taking out three of the whites) mash and mingle them well with the cream and butter: then put in the grated bread and carrot, with near half a pound of sugar, and a little salt; some grated nutmeg and beaten

spice; and pour all into a convenient dish or pan, butter'd, to keep the ingredients from sticking and burning; set it in a quick oven for about an hour, and so have you a composition for any root-pudding. *[Note the amendment recorded in the errata on p. 14.]*

27. *Penny-royal.* The cream, eggs, spice, &c. as above, but not so much sugar and salt: take a pretty quantity of peny-royal and marigold flower, &c. very well shred, and mingle with the cream, eggs, &c. four spoonfuls of sack; half a pint more of cream, and almost a pound of beef-suet chopt very small, the gratings of a two-penny loaf, and stirring all well together, put it into a bag flower'd and tie it fast. It will be boil'd within an hour: or may be baked in the pan like the carrot-pudding. The sauce is for both, a little rose-water, less vinegar, with butter beaten together and poured on it sweetned with the sugar caster.

Of this plant discreetly dried, is made a most wholsom and excellent tea.

28. Of *Spinage.* Take a sufficient quantity of spinach, stamp and strain out the juice; put to it grated manchet, the yolk of as many eggs as in the former composition of the carrot-pudding; some marrow shred small, nutmeg, sugar, some Corinths, (if you please) a few carroways, rose, or orange-flower water (as you best like) to make it grateful. Mingle all with a little boiled cream; and set the dish or pan in the oven, with a garnish of puff-paste. It will require but very moderate baking. Thus have you receits for herb puddings.

29. *Skirret-milk.* Is made by boiling the roots tender, and the pulp strained out, put into cream or new milk boiled, with three or four yolks of eggs, sugar, large mace and other spice, &c. and thus is composed any other root-milk. See *Acetar.* p. 41.

30. *Tansie.*   Take the gratings or slices of three Naples-biscuits, put them into half a pint of cream, with twelve fresh eggs, four of the whites cast out, strain the rest, and break them with two spoonfuls of rose-water, a little salt and sugar, half a grated nutmeg: and when ready for the pan, put almost a pint of the juice of spinach, cleaver, beets, corn-sallet, green corn, violet or primrose tender leaves, (for of any of these you may take your choice) with a very small sprig of tansie, and let it be fried so as to look green in the dish with a strew of sugar, and store of the juice of orange: some affect to have it fryed a little brown and crisp.

31. *Tart of herbs.*   An herb-tart is made thus: boil fresh cream or milk, with a little grated bread or Naples-biscuit (which is better) to thicken it; a pretty quantity of chervile, spinach, beete (or what other herb you please) being first par-boil'd and chop'd. Then add macaron, or almonds beaten to a paste, a little sweet butter, the yolk of five eggs, three of the whites rejected. To these some add Corinths plump'd in milk, or boil'd therein, sugar, spice at discretion, and stirring it all together over the fire, bake it in the tart-pan.

32. *Thistle.*   Take the long stalks of the middle leaf of the milky-thistle, about May, when they are young and tender: wash and scrape them, and boil them in water, with a little salt, till they are very soft, and so let them lie to drain. They are eaten with fresh butter melted not too thin, and is a delicate and wholesome dish. Other stalks of the same kind may so be treated, as the bur, being tender and disarmed of its prickles, &c.

33. *Trufles*, and other *tubers*, and *boleti*, are roasted whole in the embers; then slic'd and stew'd in strong broth with spice, &c. as mushroms are. Vide *Acetar.* p. 32.

34. *Turnep.* Take their stalks (when they begin to run up to seed) as far as they will easily break downwards: peel and tie them in bundles. Then boiling them as they do sparagus, are to be eaten with melted butter. Lastly,

35. Minc'd, or sallet-all sorts.

Take almonds blanch'd in cold water, cut them round and thin, and so leave them in the water; then have pickl'd cucumbers, olives, cornelians, capers, berberries, red-beet, buds of nasturtium, broom, &c. purslan stalk, sampier, ash-keys, walnuts, mushrooms (and almost of all the pickl'd furniture) with raisins of the sun ston'd, citron and orange-peel, Corinths (well cleansed and dried) &c. mince them severally (except the Corinths) or all together; and strew them over with any candy'd flowers, and so dispose of them in the same dish both mixt, and by themselves. To these add roasted maroons, pistachios, pine-kernels, and of almonds four times as much as of the rest, with some rose-water. Here also come in the pickled flowers and vinegar in little china dishes. And thus have you an universal winter-sallet, or an all sort in compendium, fitted for a City feast, and distinguished from the grand-sallet: which shoul'd consist of the green blanch'd and unpickled, under a stately pennash of sellery, adorn'd with buds and flowers.

And thus have we presented you a taste of our English garden housewifry in the matter of sallets: and though some of them may be vulgar, (as are most of the best things;) yet she was willing to impart them, to shew the plenty, riches and variety of the sallet-garden: and to justifie what has been asserted of the possibility of living (not unhapily) on herbs and plants, according to original and divine institution, improved by time and long experience. And if we have admitted mushroms among the rest (contrary to our intention,

and for reasons given, *Acet.* p. 32.) since many will by no means
abandon them, we have endeavoured to preserve them from those
pernicious effects which are attributed to, and really in them: we
cannot tell indeed whether they were so treated and accommodated
for the most luxurious of the Cæsarean tables, when that monarchy
was in its highest strain of epicurism, and ingross'd this haugout for
their second course; whilst this we know, that 'tis but what nature
affords all her vagabonds under every hedge.

And now, that our sallets may not want a glass of generous wine
of the same growth with the rest of the garden to recommend it, let
us have your opinion of the following.

Cowslip-wine.   To every gallon of water put two pounds of
sugar; boil it an hour, and set it to cool: then spread a good brown
toast on both sides with yeast: but before you make use of it, beat
some syrop of citron with it, an ounce and half of syrup to each gallon
of liquor: then put in the toast whilst hot, to assist its fermentation,
which will cease in two days; during which time cast in the cowslip-
flowers (a little bruised, but not much stamp'd) to the quantity of half
a bushel to ten gallons (or rather three pecks) four limons slic'd, with
the rinds and all. Lastly, one pottle of white or Rhenish wine; and
then after two days, tun it up in a sweet cask. Some leave out all the
syrup.

And here, before we conclude, since there is nothing of more
constant use than good vinegar; or that has so near an affinity to all
our *Acetaria*, we think it not amiss to add the following (much
approved) receit.

Vinegar.   To every gallon of spring water let there be
allowed three pounds of Malaga-raisins: put them in an earthen jarr,
and place them where they may have the hottest sun, from May till
Michaelmas: then pressing them well, tun the liquor up in a very

strong iron-hoop'd vessel to prevent its bursting. It will appear very thick and muddy when newly press'd, but will refine in the vessel, and be as clear as wine. Thus let it remain untouched for three months, before it be drawn off, and it will prove excellent vinegar.

Butter. Butter being likewise so frequent and necessary an ingredient to divers of the foregoing appendants: it should be carefully melted, that it turn not to an oil; which is prevented by melting it leisurely, with a little fair water at the bottom of the dish or pan; and by continual shaking and stirring, kept from boiling or over-heating, which makes it rank.

Other rare and exquisite liquors and teas (products of our gardens only) we might superadd, which we leave to our lady housewives, whose province indeed all this while it is.

THE
TABLE

[This index, compiled by Evelyn or his assistant, is printed as in the original edition, save the Greek words have been transliterated (in small capitals), and the page references have been made to agree with the present version. Where a reference was clearly misplaced, it has been corrected.]

111

Preparation to the dressing, of sallets,
16,64
Prodigal, 53
PSUCHRAI, 16
Pugil, 59
Punishment, 26
Purslan, 37
Putrefaction, 35,41
Pythagoras, 76

Quality and virtue of plants, 48
see Plants

Radish, 37
of gold dedicated at Delphi, 38
Moschius wrote a whole volume in
praise of them, *ib.*
Hippocrates condemns them, *ib.*
Raphanus rusticanus horse-radish, 38
Radix lunaria, 45
personata, 45
Ragout, 32
Rampion, 39
Rapum, 43
Ray, Mr.,49, 85
Refreshing, 22,27,35
Restaurative, 18,20,43,47
Rocket, 39
Roccombo, 26
Roman sallet, 86
lux[ury], 88,89
Rosemary, 39
Roots, 37
Rhue, 45

Saffron, 57
Sage, 39
Sallets, what, how improved, whence
so called, 16
ingredients, 17
variety and store above what the
ancients had, 86,87
bills of fare, 86

Sallets, cont.
skill in choosing, gathering,
composing and dressing,
45,48,49,50,51,54,58,61,64
found in crops of foul, 54
what formerly in use, now
abdicated, 45
extemporary sallets, 70
whether best to begin or conclude
with sallets, 61
Salade de preter, 22
Salt, 56
what best for sallets, 56
salts essential, and of vegetables,
56,57
Sambucus, 24
Sampier, 39
Sanguine, 37
Sarcophagists, 50
Sauce, 38,64
Savoys, 21
Scallions, 40
Scorbute, *vide* Scurvy
Scurvy-grass, 40
Scurvy, 20,23,33,38,41,51
Season, 60,68
Seasoning, 65
vide Sallet
Sedum minus, 43
vide Stone-crop
Sellery, 40,64
Seneca, 77
Shambles, 64,66,69,86,91
Sight45,48
vide Eyes
Silphium, 46
how precious and sacred, 46
Simples, 45
Sinapi, 33
Sisarum, 40
Skirrits, *ib.*
Sleep, to procure, 27
Smallage, 40
Smut in wheat, 69

APPENDIX

Containing receits for the pickling and other ways of accommodating winter-
sallets.

Artichoks.	Nasturtium.
Ashen-keys.	Orange.
Asparagus.	Parsnip.
Beans.	Peny-royal.
Beet.	Potato.
Broom-buds.	Purselan.
Carrot.	Radish.
Champignons.	Sampier.
Chessnuts.	Skirret.
Cauly-flowers.	Spinach.
Cowslips.	Spinach.
Cucumber.	Tansie.
Elder-flowers.	Thistle.
Gilliflowers.	Vinegar.
Herbs.	Wine.
Limons.	Turnip.
Melon.	Walnuts.
Mushrom.	Butter.
Mustard.	

FINIS.

INDEX & GLOSSARY

Foreign names of plants used by Evelyn are indexed where they occur. Their modern English equivalents are given in round brackets. Otherwise, plants are indexed by their usual modern English name, and the current botanical name is given in square brackets. Authors and authorities (except the Bible) have been indexed and identified where possible, but the titles of their respective books have not been included. Words in the text that may cause the modern reader recourse to a large historical dictionary have been incorporated in this index with a brief definition, but no page reference. Subjects have been only lightly indexed; the reader is directed to Evelyn's own index for guidance. Entries are by and large to substantive occurrences in the text. Ingredients of recipes, for example, are not indexed.

Augustus (63 BC–AD 14), emperor, 27
Averroës (1126–1198), philosopher, 16,20
Bacon, Francis, Lord Verulam, Viscount St
Albans (1561–1626), philosopher,
33,67,72,95
Bacon, Roger (1214–1292) philosopher, 69
Balm, baum [*Melissa officinalis*], 19; salt, 55
Barlæus, Caspar (fl. 1638), Dutch poet, 87
Bartholinus, Thomas (1616–1680), Danish
physician, 80
Basil [*Ocimum basilicum*], 19
Baskets, 58
Battus, founder of the city of Cyrene, 46
Bauhin, Jean (1541–1613) Swiss botanist, 47
Beans, French [*Phaseolus vulgaris*], pickled,
99
Beans, haricot [*Phaseolus vulgaris*], pickled,
61,99
Bed-bug, see Wall-louse [*Cimex*]
Beet [*Beta vulgaris*], 19; sea [*Beta vulgaris*
ssp. *maritima*], 19
Bellis-major (Daisy), 24
Benzoin, 47
Berberry, barberry [*Berberis vulgaris*],
pickled, 61
Beta (Beet), 19
Beverovicius, John, 71
Blite [*Chenopodium bonus-henricus*], 19
Blitum (Blite), 19
Blondel, Blundel, David (1591–1655),
French protestant, 81
Bochart, Samuel (1599–1667), French
theologian, 81
Bohemian red turnip, 43
Boletus, 31
roasted and stewed, 107
Bologna, Bolognia (Italy), fennel, 25
Bontius, 46
Bonus henricus (English mercury), see Blite
Borage, borrage [*Borago officinalis*], 20
Borrago (Borage), 20
Boyle, Robert (1627–1691), scientist, 58,95
Brahmins, Bramins, 46,76
Brassica (Cabbage), 21

Bread, turnip, 43
Broccoli, Calabrese, 21
Brooklime [*Veronica beccabunga*], 20
Broom [*Saronthamnus scoparius*], buds or
pods, 20; pickled, 61,99
Browne, Sir Thomas (1605–1682), author, 69
Budæus (Budé), Jo., 47
Buds, 20
Bugloss [*Anchusa italica*], 20
Buglossum (Bugloss), 20,25
Bulbo-castanum (Earth-nut), 24
Buphthalmum (Ox-eye daisy), 24
Burdock [*Arctium lappa*], 46
Burnet saxifrage [*Pimpinella saxifraga*], 36;
pepper, 57
Butter, 110

Cabbage [*Brassica oleracea*], 21; Savoy, 21
Cabinet, summer-house or bower
Caesar, Julius (100–44 BC), 46
Cajetan, Cardinal (1469–1534), 81
Calvin, John (1509–1564), 81
Campanula, esculent, see Rampion
Capellus, Jac., 81
Capers [*Capparis spinosa*], 20,61
Capitata marina & florida (Seakale), 21
Capreols, tendrils
Capsicum, Indian [*Capsicum annuum*], 36
Capuchin capers, nasturtium seeds, 23; see
also Nasturtium
Cardan, Jerome (Hieronymus Cardanus)
(1501–1576), Italian scientist, 48,67,71
Cardialgium, heartburn or indigestion
Cardoon, cardon, chardoon [*Cynara
cardunculus*], 46; Spanish, 18
Carduus Mariæ (Milk thistle), 42
Carduus sativus (Cardoon), 18
Carrot [*Daucus carota*], 22
pudding, 105
Carthage, 18
Cartucci (Celery), 25
Casaubon, Isaac (1559–1614), French
humanist, 30
Cato, the Elder (234–149 BC), 21

Culpeper, Nicholas (1616–1654), writer on astrology and medicine, 60

Cumini sectores, splitters of hairs (*cumini*=cumin seeds)

Curcellæus, 80

Curly endive, see Endive

Cutlery for preparing salads, 58

Cymae, cimae, cimata, heads or buds

Cyrene, North Africa, 46

Daffodil [*Narcissus pseudonarcissus*], 44

Daisy [*Bellis perennis*], 24

Dandelion [*Taraxacum officinale*], 24

Dappled thistle, see Thistle, milk

Dauci (Carrots), 22

Dedals, cunning conceits

Delphi, Greece, 46

Democritus (460–c.357 BC), Greek philosopher, 52

Denmark, cabbage seed from, 21

Dens leonis (Dandelion), 24

Depurate, to purify

Detersive, cleansing, detergent

Digby, Sir Kenelm (1603–1665), diplomatist and writer, 95

Dionysius Carthusianus, 80

Dioscorides [Dioscurides] (1st century AD), Greek physician, 8,29,38

Diphilus of Siphnos, Greek writer on diet, 19,67,71

Dishes, for salads, 58

Dock [*Rumex*], 24; sharp-pointed, 24

Dodonæus, 45

Dog's mercury [*Mercurialis perennis*], 48

Domitian (AD 51–96), Roman emperor, 62

Dover, Kent, 39,104

Draco herba (Tarragon), 42

Dracontium, 45

Dressing, salad, 60-5, *et passim*

Dutch asparagus, 41

Earth-nuts, earthnuts [*Conopodium majus*], 24

Edulcorated, sweetened, softened

Edule, plants that are eaten, edible

Eggs, 57,86

Egypt, onions in, 34

Egyptians, ancient, 71,76

Elaboratory, laboratory

Elder [*Sambucus niger*], 24, 25; pickle, 100; vinegar, 55

Embamma, appetising sauce in which articles of food were dipped before being administered as medicine

Encarpa, architectural ornament of festoons of fruit

Endive [*Cichorium endivia, Cichorium intybus*], 24

Endivium (Endive), 24

English Mercury [*Chenopodium bonus-henricus*], 19

Epimenedes (6th century BC), Cretan poet, 29

Eringo, eryngo, see Sea holly

Eruca (Rocket), 39

Esculent, edible

Essex, 65

Eubulus (4th century BC), Athenian statesman, 27

Euphrosynum (Bugloss), 20

Eupolis (5th century BC), Greek playwright, 88

Euripides (c.485–406 BC), 31

Eusebius (c.AD 260–c.340), Greek Christian writer, 76

Faber, Honoratus, 70

Fennel, fennil [*Foeniculum vulgare* var. *dulce*], 25,40,48

Fernel, Jean François (1497–1558), French mathematician and physician, 27

Feuillantine order of nuns, 82

Flowers, 25

Fœniculum (Fennel), 25

Fœtid assa, see Asafœtida

Foxglove, see Poppy, green

Uliginous, swampy
Urtica (Nettle), 33

Valentinian I (AD 321–375), emperor, 83
Valerian family of Rome, 27,89
Valerianella (Corn salad), 22
Varro (116–27 BC), author, 15
Verjuice, 55
Verulam, Baron, see Bacon, Nicholas
Vine, see Grapevine
Vinegar, 55,109, *et passim*; see also under
  names of types
Viola matronalis, 45
Viper-grass [*Scorzonera hispanica*], see
  Scorzonera
Virgil (70–19 BC), poet, 62
Vitis (Grapevine), 43
Vopiscus, Flavius (4th century AD), supposed
  joint-author of *Historia Augusta,* 27
Vossius, Gerard Jan (1577–1649), Dutch
  scholar, 81

Wales, leeks in, 27
Wall-louse [*Cimex*], 49
Walnut, wall-nut [*Juglans regia*], 36; mango
  of, 104-5; pickled, 61,104
Watercress [*Nasturtium officinale*], 23
Wiburg St Giles, see Wimborne St Giles
Wild thyme, see Thyme
Wimborne St Giles, Dorset, 21
Winders, the clinging stalks of goosegrass
  (?fr. whin, furze, gorse or grasses), 22
Wine, baulm, 19; cowslip, 19,109
Winter cress [*Barbarea verna*], 23
Winter salad, 108
Wood-sorrel [*Oxalis acetosella*], 44
Wormwood [*Artemisia absinthum*], 45; salt,
  55
Xenocrates (fl. 339 BC), Greek philosopher,
  76
Yorkshire mustard seed, 56
Zanchy, 81
Zeno (c. 490–445 BC), Greek philosopher, 76